Seeking God:
Understanding the Bible
and Christianity

Seeking God:
Understanding the Bible and Christianity

Edward F. LeGault

Seeking God:
Understanding the Bible
and Christianity

ISBN-13: 978-0615662152

ISBN-10: 0615662153

Second Edition

Serenity Valley Publishing
Shelton, Washington, USA

www.SerenityValleyPublishing.com

There are many people I would like to thank:

Fern, for all those summer Bible School classes at the Buck's Prairie Grange Hall, in what seems like a long, long time ago;

Johnny, from our time on the USS Nimitz for his showing me that a sailor could be a Christian and still have a good time ashore;

Gary, for being a great Navy buddy and my "best man";

Our dear friend and my former co-worker Kathleen for those lunch hours of racquetball and then her pointing me in the right direction towards God (...and introducing me to my eventual bride!);

The guys at San Jose Careers Alive for keeping watch over one another;

Pastor Ron for his letter of recommendation to help me get into San Jose Christian College... and also for letting me preach my first sermons;

My friends in our San Jose Christian College/William Jessup University cohort group;

The *very* reverend Sam for being our cohort mentor and professor at SJCC/WJU (and the guy who got me out of my shyness shell);

And last, but not least, my lovely wife Nila and my beautiful daughter Kathleen for all their encouragement and support ("...and *which* book is this you are working on now?...")

This book is dedicated to my friend John Dawson.
John was always there to help us when we needed it. He
knows Christ as a personal friend and Savior.
- RIP -

Serenity Valley is more of an attitude
or way of life... than an actual location.

Table of Contents

Foreword

Finding God   1
In The Beginning   7
God's Contract   9
God's Law   15
The Royal Lineage   21
Translations vs Versions   27
Problems With Translations   31
The Old Testament's Roots   33
The New Testament's Roots   35
Translating The Bible   39
Interpreting The Bible   43
Applying Scripture   55
What Christians Believe   61
Atonement   65
Who is Jesus?   69
Faith   73
The Gospels   81
Harmony Of The Gospels   83
Leadership   85
Fatherhood   91
State Of The Christian Church   111
Prayer   115
Why do bad things happen to good people?   119
Doxology   125
Appendixes   127

Foreword

This book did not just happen. I truly believe it was planned by God. I hope I didn't disappoint Him too much. The beginnings of the writings between these covers started a few years ago when I was a student at San Jose Christian College. I had been laid off, or RIF'd, from a large computer company. I was seeking something to do with the rest of my adult life. I was trying to find a new job and everywhere I turned I was told I needed a college-level Bachelor's degree in *anything* to get past the various corporate Human Relations gate keepers. No matter that I had several years of experience and years of technical training. No college degree, no job interview.

One day, while driving down the street, I heard an advertisement on the radio about a two-year, night-class, college completion program and decided to give it a try… That was, without doubt, some of the best twenty-six months of my life. We studied hard. We learned. We "un-learned." We learned a lot about God, the Bible, each other and ourselves. Our cohort group had fun times, sad times and many, many hours of learning from some of the best theology minds in the greater San Jose (CA) area. We did a great deal of writing – our weekly class assignments and class finals were all accomplished by reading, thinking and writing. A lot of writing.

Skip ahead a few years. I was looking through my computer archives and stumbled upon all my writings for those SJCC classes. Then I was in church one day, before the service, and talking with someone about the need for a book or study material for those seeking information about God, the Bible and Christianity. Later, I was sitting in church during the worship (music/singing) phase or ceremony and realized I had a treasure trove of writings about those subjects. So, I read and re-read my writings from those college years, found some Bible studies I had written, and dug out a few sermons I had written. I decided I had about ninety percent of the material needed for a book. It turned out, like many other projects, once I got into it, I learned I had ninety percent done and about ninety percent to go!

This book is not meant to be a Bible commentary. It is not meant to be the ultimate scholarship or authority on the Bible or Christianity. And it is certainly not a road map to becoming a Christian. These words contained here are simply the story of one seeker's journey to a deeper understanding of God and His universe. This work was originally mostly a series of essays in various lengths from one paragraph to several pages. It was never meant to become a book. At least, *not by me*. It is said that **God works in mysterious ways**. I believe that with all my heart and mind. No one person is an absolute expert on God. If they say they are – run quickly away! I just strive to understand Him, His Son, and the Holy Spirit a little bit better. Enjoy my writings. I hope you learn a little more than you knew before you started. I pray it makes you curious enough to want to go out there to really find out more about the Bible, Christianity, and God. Here then is a book for those seeking God, and/or trying to understand, or just thinking about what this Bible and Christianity thing is all about.

And a final note: I am a college graduate and really do know how to use proper grammar. This book has mostly been taken from a series of boring college essays and converted to how I speak… Think of this book as a series of talks or mini-sermons and ignore the poor grammar found in some places...

Section One:

Seeking God

Chapter One
Finding God

I found God. I wasn't really looking for Him. It didn't happen at any place I would have expected to find Him. It just happened one day. It was kind of easy. Not like a friend of mine who found God in a street gutter. Or a guy I read about who found God in a bowl of soup. I didn't have to lose everything and be at the bottom of my life physically or emotionally. Amazing things can happen when you least expect it. Here, then, is my story.

I grew up in a poor family in the Pacific Northwest. My dad was a gyppo logger (independent, small operations "gypsy" logger). My mom was mostly a housewife, but she worked as needed when the logging business wasn't bringing in the income for a family with four children to feed and clothe. As the oldest child, I didn't think I had the parenting leeway my younger siblings had growing up. Since I was the first child, I was the great experiment for behavior, school, etc. Then I got old enough in high school to decide to take control of my life.

We did not attend church regularly. In my very early

childhood my family intermittantly attended a Catholic church, and then later we became Lutherans. Long story. Not really relevant to *this* story. I like to say I was born a Catholic, then baptized a Lutheran when a teenager, and finally as an adult many years later, I became a Christian.

One of the reasons we weren't in church a lot on Sundays is because we spent a great deal of time in the great outdoors camping, fishing and hunting. Even after Dad had spent the week working in the woods, he still wanted to get outside to relax. As the oldest child, my dad would ask me my opinion about where to go fishing, hunting, etc. Making decisions was really awesome.

I learned to make decisions for a lot of things. I figured I could make decisions to control my own life:

- I could decide how well I would do in high school.
- I could decide what college to attend.
- I could decide what to study in college and how well I would do.
- When I decided to drop out of college I could decide what to do for the rest of my life.
- Like where to work.
- When I couldn't decide what to do for a living, then I could enlist in the military services.
- My dad encouraged me to try the Air Force, but I decided to enlist in the Navy, instead.

And that is where the next phase of my life started.

I enlisted in the U.S. Navy at the age of twenty-three. Most of the other recruits in my boot camp company at the San Diego Recruit Training Facility were right out of high school: 17 to

19 years of age. Not only was I older than most, but I had a guaranteed rank and schools upon graduation. I had chosen wisely and made some good career decisions. I was in charge again. Then the first morning in the boot camp barracks arrived and my whole world was tossed upside down. With about three hours sleep, we were woken up by some guys in uniform banging metal garbage cans against the ends of our metal racks (bunk beds). Well, I survived boot camp. Even learned how to sleep standing up when no one was looking!

After boot camp graduation and more technical training in electricity and electronics, logic (!) and computer electronics, I was shipped off to the fleet. I became part of the crew of the brand new, nuclear powered, first in its class, the aircraft carrier USS Nimitz, CVAN 68 (later to become just CVN 68 – it's a Navy thing). I was part of Operations Department, OE Division. I met and worked with a bunch of really great guys. Met a few officers that were OK, and a few that I didn't think knew their feet from their backside (to say it really nicely). I studied hard, passed some tests, got some really good recommendations, and made the enlisted rank of E-5 (Second Class Petty Officer), then E-6 (First Class Petty Officer) and was on my way to making E-7 (Chief Petty Officer). Even had some officers try to convince me to go back to college on a special Navy program to become an officer. I thought about it and I decided that I, *and not the Navy*, was going to control my life. So, I said no, and got out of the Navy soon after that when my enlistment was up. Moved back to the West Coast and looked for a job.

I found a job with a company in Seattle. The parent company was actually in Suwanee, GA. I arrived there for the first Monday of class and they handed out a list of company rules and regulations covering behavior both on the job *and* off the job. "What do you mean I can't play video games on my own time not during working hours?" And many more rules – too numerous to list here. I made my decision – after all, I was in control of my life – and called a taxi and was on the next flight out of Georgia, back to Seattle.

I then decided I would go back to school. I enrolled in a new college in Olympia, WA – *The Evergreen State College*. I applied for my G.I. Bill Education benefits, but the Veterans' Administration dragged their feet and wasn't too keen on a brand new school, so I decided to find a new job. Landed one at a very small high tech firm based in Sunnyvale, CA. That was a great job. I worked out of my home in the Seattle area. My boss was in California. I did my own scheduling, made my own appointments and travel arrangements. I traveled across and around Canada and the western United States on business. In reality, I was pretty much my own boss. Somehow, through a set of company changes and my decision making, I ended up living and working in San Jose, CA.

The company had a corporate membership at a local health club. I learned to play racquetball. One of my regular challengers on the courts was a young lady who was a self-taught computer programmer at our work. We played an occasional game of racquetball... and she did not beat me too badly. We would usually play during a long lunch time and then actually have lunch afterward at a local eating establishment. Yes, we occasionally took long lunch hours, but we also worked hard: 12+ hour days were not abnormal.

One day after a game of racquetball we stopped to eat at a local restaurant. I was driving a pickup truck with a shell, or canopy, on the back. I had found a shaded spot in the parking lot and we both got out of the truck, on opposite sides. I heard a loud *CRACK!* sound and looked up to see this huge piece of the tree in front of my truck falling out of the sky directly on my dear friend. My mouth was open, but I could not even yell a warning. At that moment I realized here was something I could NOT control. *I could not fix it.* Nothing I could do. Nada. So, for the first time in my life I asked God for protection and help for a friend. Miraculously (and I do mean it was a *real* miracle), she somehow was not there under the fallen tree. I ran around the truck to find the tree had fallen right where she had been standing. She did not know how she got out from under the falling tree. I knew. **God** had done it. And *without any help from me.*

We went on to have lunch at the restaurant and we talked a lot about God, Jesus and the Bible. I decided I would read the Bible from beginning to end. So I did. Some of the books of the Old Testament got a little dry and sleepy. But, over a series of months, I did read the Bible as best I could. I joined a couple Bible studies and learned I would never know everything about God, Jesus and the Holy Spirit. The Bible is a wonderful, amazing book.

Edward F. LeGault

Chapter 2
In The Beginning

Have you ever looked through a microscope at a drop of water? It's kind of scary. Water is teeming with life. And if you magnify those little critters swimming around they look like weird monsters from some science fiction movie.

How about going outside on a clear night? Look up at the lights in the sky. Without the help of a telescope you will see thousands of stars, and a couple planets if you are lucky. Not counting the moon and artificial satellites orbiting the Earth, there are masses of lights to see. The stars, the lights of the Milky Way, and much more. Add a telescope to your viewing and there are millions, make that billions, of stars to see.

Astronomers and physicists tell us billions of years ago the entire universe existed as a super compact mass the size of a golf ball. Then it exploded with a big bang, forming the universe as we know it. Funny thing about that big bang theory – ask those same scientists what caused that explosion, or even where that super compact golf ball sized matter and energy came from, and they just shrug their shoulders and say

Edward F. LeGault

"it just happened". They even tell us the big bang occurred **everywhere** at the same time. And they tell us it happened a finite amount of time ago – about 13 billion years ago. Well, what then existed before the big bang?

In the beginning, God created the heavens and the earth (Genesis 1:1).

Or, to put it in terms my scientist friends would understand it: In the beginning, <u>with a really, really big bang</u>, God created the heavens and the Earth, everywhere at the same time.

As I studied the Bible and started to learn about God, I became convinced God has always existed and always will. Very hard to get hold of that philosophical idea, but there it is.

We are now going to bounce around the Old Testament to try to get an understanding of God and life from an Israelite or Jewish, point of view.

Chapter 3
God's Contract

In the beginning, God created the Heavens and the Earth.
Adam and Eve had a good life in the Garden of Eden. Good
weather, free food, and God walked and talked with them in
the Garden. God provided for all of their needs. God had told
them not to eat the fruit of the Tree of Knowledge. They did
not obey God and suffered the consequences of their sin.

Expelled from the Garden of Eden they learned to work for
their provisions. And that was all new to the two of them.
They had to find or build shelter. Farming skills and
techniques had to be invented and perfected. There was the
problem of protection from the unfriendly wild animals.
Children must have been a really big surprise and a new
responsibility. People do what people do and succumbed to
sinful ways, including murder and worshipping false idols.

Several generations later God cleansed the Earth of sinful
people through the Great Flood. The only survivors were the
faithful and righteous Noah and his family, along with the
animals and birds Noah rescued. God then made a covenant,

or contractual promise with Noah never again to destroy the Earth with flood waters. So now, no matter how hard it rains or floods, I know the end of the Earth is not coming from another great flood! God gave us rainbows after a rain to remind us of His promise.

Several more generations later, as told in the twelfth chapter of Genesis, God told Abram to leave his country, his people and his father's household. God was sending Abram to another land. In Genesis 12:2-3 we learn of the seven promises God made to Abram:

- "I will make you into a great nation.
- I will bless you.
- I will make your name great.
- You will be a blessing.
- I will bless those who bless you.
- Whoever curses you I will curse.
- All peoples on earth will be blessed through you."

In chapter 15 of Genesis, we are told Abram had a vision and the Word of God came to him. God informed Abram his offspring would be as numerous as the stars in the night sky. God told Abram to bring a heifer, a goat, a ram, a dove, and a pigeon. Abram prepared the animals and birds for a covenantal sacrifice (Note: Covenant = a contract guaranteed with a blood sacrifice by two parties). However, God Himself passed between the sacrificial pieces for **both** parties of the contract (God and Abram) and on that day He made a blood covenant, or promise, to Abram. He told Abram He would give that land to his descendants. This implied that Abram, who was over 75 years old, would father a child. Abram and his wife Sarai had little faith in God's promise and then took matters into their own plan. Sarai substituted her younger

Egyptian maidservant Hagar to bear Abram a child when he was 86 years old (Abram *should* have known better!). But this was not according to God's plan. God had made a covenant, or promise, to Abram (and Sarai). When Abram was 99 years old God appeared to him again. God reaffirmed his covenant with Abram.

Abram would now be known as Abraham and his wife Sarai would now be known as Sarah. God established an additional covenant, or contract, of circumcision. Every male of Abraham's family, clan, or household slaves would be circumcised to establish an agreement of their flesh sacrifice with God's promise. God promised Abraham a child through his legal wife Sarah. Isaac was eventually born of them. Abraham was reminded that God can do what He promises. Nothing is too difficult for the Lord. Even though Isaac was the second born (son of Sarai/Sarah) of Abraham, he would inherit the covenant between God and his father.

When Isaac was forty years old he married Rebekah, daughter of Bethuel. Rebekah, like the history of Isaac's mother, was barren. However, Isaac did not turn to a handmaiden or concubine for a substitute mother of his offspring. Isaac prayed to the Lord on behalf of his wife. Rebekah eventually became pregnant and gave birth to twins Esau and Jacob. There came a famine in the land and the Lord God appeared to Isaac. He told Isaac to not go to Egypt, but to stay where he was. God reaffirmed His covenant made with Isaac's father, Abraham, by telling Isaac He would be with him, bless him, give him all the lands he saw there, his descendants would be as numerous as the stars in the sky, and through his first born offspring all nations on earth would be blessed. Instead, Jacob, the second born of Isaac, would get the blessing of his father through deception.

Edward F. LeGault

Esau held a grudge against his brother Jacob for losing his firstborn birthright to him through a deceptive ploy (good reading in the Old Testament).

Jacob fled to Haran to live with his mother's brother, Laban. Before he departed his father, Isaac gave him a blessing and told him not to marry a Canaanite woman, but recommended he take a wife from among Laban's daughters. On his journey to Haran, Jacob had a dream in which God told him He was the Lord of Abraham and Isaac. Jacob's descendants were to be as numerous as dust of the earth, would get the land on which he was lying, and all the peoples of the earth would be blessed through him and his offspring. God promised to watch over and protect him until this was done. Jacob continued on to Haran. Jacob fell in love with Rachel, one of Laban's daughters, but then *he* was deceived into first marrying Leah, her older sister.

In chapter 35 of Genesis, we learn God told Jacob to return to Bethel. God also gave Jacob a new name of Israel. Again, God reaffirms His promise to Abraham that the land promised to Abraham and Isaac would belong to Jacob and His descendants.

In chapter 46 of Genesis, Jacob and his family set out for Egypt to visit his son Joseph. Again, Jacob had a vision of God. God tells Jacob to go to Egypt where He would make them a great nation there. Jacob took all his offspring with him to Egypt. Eventually the king of Egypt dies and the Israelites fall out of favor with the Pharaoh.

Later in history, Moses, a Hebrew who was raised by a Pharaoh's family loses his temper, kills an Egyptian, and flees to Midian for his life. In the third chapter of Exodus, it is written how one day while Moses was tending the flock of his father-in-law, the priest of Midian, an angel of the Lord appeared to him in a burning bush. God sends Moses back to Egypt to bring His people out of slavery. In chapter six of Exodus, God tells Moses of the covenant He established with Abraham, Isaac and Jacob. God told Moses He would redeem His Hebrew people with mighty acts of judgments against Pharaoh. God's redeeming promise would bring freedom and joy to the Israelites. The Israelites, however, would repeatedly turn their backs on the Lord and would suffer the consequences of their actions.

In the New Testament, Romans chapters four and five record the Apostle Paul's words concerning Abraham's faith. We are reminded that Abraham was justified before God by his righteousness *before* he was circumcised. **Faith**, not the Law, was the reason God blessed Abraham and his descendants. Without the sacrifice of God's own son, we would have to pay with our own lives in order to be justified by God to pay for our own sins. However, we have now been justified through Christ's death. Our own sins have been paid by the blood of God's only son. Galatians 3:6 tells us "Abraham believed God and it was credited to him as righteousness. Therefore, those who believe (in Jesus Christ) are the children of Abraham." God told Abraham that even the Gentiles would be His people ("...all nations would be blessed through you..."). The Apostle Luke recognized this when he wrote, in Acts 3:24-25, of the prophesy where all peoples would be blessed through Abraham's offspring.

God *always* has had a plan for our salvation and blessings.

The patriarchs of the Old Testament had *just a part* of God's plan revealed to them. They had to live a righteous life in order to receive God's blessings and salvation. *We* now have the advantage of Christ's sacrifice which pays for our sins. **Faith in Jesus Christ**, as our Savior, will redeem us before God's eyes. This is the New (blood) Covenant, or New Testament, from our Lord God. It is that simple… there is nothing mysterious or difficult in receiving eternal salvation!

Chapter 4
God's Law

What is "worship"?
Is it a ritual, or a ceremony?
Is it an attitude, or part of a belief?
Is it something personal, or is it something done by groups,
congregations, or even whole communities?

In my Old Testament studies I found the Greek word *latreia*
and the Hebrew word *abodah* used in reference to worship.
Both words seem to have originally referred to the labor of
hired servants or slaves. Servants and slaves are meant to
obey their master for the master's pleasure. *Worship* should be
a matter of doing things to bring pleasure to our master, God.

Abraham had certainly known of this custom and necessity of
worshiping God. Worshiping God, or even worshiping local
pagan gods, goes back to the earliest recorded history. In
Genesis chapter 4, we have an early reference to Cain and
Abel making an offering to the Lord. God looked with favor
on Abel because of his fat portions offering from some of his
firstborn animal flocks. God did not like Cain's fruits and

vegetables offering. From the earliest times God has preferred a choice: a generous offering which takes some work and energy over a careless, thoughtless offering made with little effort on the part of the worshiper.

After the great Flood, Noah built an alter and made a sacrifice of burnt offerings to the Lord from some of all the clean animals and clean birds he had just spent a great deal of effort and time saving from destruction. In both of these examples, God is separate from the worshiper. I believe God means for worship to take some time and effort on the part of the worshiper (me, us) -- not just always to be a quick thank you or an emergency request to Him.

Sacrificial offerings seemed to have been made either at the request of God or as special one-time acts to God as a matter of thanksgiving. In chapter 22 of Genesis, Abraham is told by God to take Isaac, his only (legal) son (of Sarah) to the region of Moriah and sacrifice him there as a burnt offering. Abraham and Isaac were certainly familiar with burnt offering sacrifices. Abraham also knew God had promised him a great line of descendants through Isaac, but yet God had just told him to take his son up on the mountain, slit his throat, and then burn his freshly slaughtered remains! Abraham had the faith and patience necessary to trust that God would provide the real animal for the burnt offering.

Isaac, as a volunteer participant, surely had a great amount of faith in God – after all, he was heading up the mountain for a ceremony which could have been the end of his young life! Abraham was willing to give up his most precious treasure, his son's life, to the Lord. (Just as later God would give his own Son as a sacrifice for us).

On a side note, I believe this was a significant episode in the development of burnt offerings in human religious history. God made it clear it was *not* necessary for man to sacrifice humans. God could have let Abraham sacrifice Isaac and provided him another son through Sarah or used Ishmael for his purposes, or even brought Isaac back to life. But we know **God has a plan**. God is still separate and distant from mankind at that time, but yet we see him work in the lives of His faithful followers.

In the book of Exodus, Moses encountered God close-up in the form of an angel of the Lord contained in the flames of a burning bush. God told Moses of His plans to get His people out of slavery from Egypt. Not only was God speaking to the faithful, such as Moses and Aaron, but God came into Moses' close proximity. Moses was afraid to look directly at God and hid his face. Moses was able to lead God's people out of Egypt only after a series of plagues placed upon Pharaoh by God.

The final plague, of death, to the firstborns of Egypt was avoided by the Israelites through their sacrificing first born lambs and painting their blood on the sides and tops of their door frames. This is, still to this day, celebrated as the Jewish holy day *Passover.*

During the wanderings of the Israelites in the wilderness, God descended to the top of Mount Sinai and called Moses up to the mountain. There, Moses received the Ten Commandments from God. And, God again warned the Israelites not to have any other gods or idols alongside Him. In chapter 20 of Exodus, God commanded them to build altars to Him only of dirt or undressed stones for burnt offerings. In chapter 23 of Genesis, God added the community celebrations of the Feast of Unleavened Bread, the Feast of the Harvest, and the Feast of In-gatherings to the Israelites' annual calendar.

Then the Lord led the Israelites in their wanderings through the wilderness, along with more warnings to avoid the local pagan gods and deities they would encounter. Later, in chapters 25 - 26 of Genesis, God gave instructions on how to build the Ark of the Covenant and the Tabernacle tent. The presence of the Lord would reside within the Ark inside the most holy inner part of the Tabernacle. Originally, the Tabernacle tent was set up outside the main tent encampment of the Israelites. Moses would go out to it to meet with God.

Later the tent Tabernacle was set up by the Levite priests in the center of their encampments. The ordinary people were then able to have a more close experience with God's presence. Off and on, the peoples of some of the Israelite tribes departed from God's teachings and intermarried with foreigners. This usually meant they adopted the foreigners' pagan gods and idols. God then became displeased and the Israelites suffered the consequences of their actions.

King David united the tribes in the Promised Land with a centralized government in Jerusalem. After building his personal palace he desired to build a permanent temple for God (and the Ark of the Covenant) in place of the semi-permanent tent Tabernacle in use at that time. Because of David's sins, it was his son Solomon who built the first permanent temple. The Temple in Jerusalem then became the central place of worship for the Jews. The Temple was destroyed and rebuilt a couple times. The Ark of the Covenant disappeared during a foreign conquest of Jerusalem. What then happened to the presence of God? The Jews were then worshiping an empty Temple. This is like worshiping idols or empty altars of other gods instead of worshiping directly to the Almighty God.

During the exile of the Jews from Israel (and Jerusalem) they needed some other place to worship God. The *synagogue* was therefore used as a meeting place for prayer and teaching God's word. There does not seem to be a definitive answer as to the origin of the synagogue. We find a reference in Psalm 74:8 to synagogues. The houses or meeting places of the prophets might have been referred to as synagogues. Synagogues originally would have been places of teaching and some prayer.

Before the Ark of the Covenant disappeared from the Temple in Jerusalem, it (the Temple) would have been the only true place to worship God because His presence resided within the Ark (in the room at the back of the Temple). After the Ark of the Covenant disappeared and the Jews were dispersed, they most likely used a meeting place, or synagogue, as their place of teaching and prayer. The Temple was rebuilt in Jerusalem, but it lacked the Ark of the Covenant. Most of the Bible references to synagogues are in the New Testament.

The crucifixion and resurrection of Jesus Christ changed the whole scope of worshiping God. The curtain in the Temple, separating the most holy inner room from the people, *was torn from the ceiling during an earthquake when Jesus died*. This signifies that God does not mean to be separated from the ordinary worshipers. The peoples of all the nations now have the opportunity to worship God *personally* and have the presence of the Holy Spirit dwell inside of each person. We can worship God individually or come together in groups. *We do not need a special building or location to worship*. Since God is with us in the form of the Holy Spirit, our *temple is*

Edward F. LeGault

with us at all times. We are our temple. The final Temple will be our everlasting life together in Heaven with God.

Chapter 5
The Royal Lineage

I am going to condense a lot of the Old Testament lineage down to a few paragraphs. The ultimate purpose is to show the "royal" lineage leading to the birth of Jesus Christ.

Jacob had twelve sons. Reuben, Simeon, Levi, Judah, Issachar, and Zebulun were born to Jacob's wife Leah. Dan and Naphtali were born to Rachel's maidservant Bilhah. Joseph and Benjamin were finally born to Jacob's number two wife (but his favorite lady), Rachel. Gad and Asher were born to Leah's maidservant Zilpah. Jacob's blessing on his sons gives us some clues as to what would happen to the future tribes of Israel. I will not even go into the differences in culture back then, versus now, when looking at all the children born to women other than Jacob's wives! Bad enough to have multiple wives (but that was OK by their clannish culture).

Reuben's descendants were characterized by indecision and cursed for Reuben's incestuous relationship with Bilhah, the mother of two of Jacob's sons.

Edward F. LeGault

Simeon and Levi are cursed for their traits of violence, anger and cruelty. Their tribes were to be dispersed throughout Israel.

Judah is blessed with the prophesy of his brothers' tribes bowing down to his lineage. Judah's descendants are to become the leaders of all the tribes.

Zebulun would live by the seashore.

Issachar would be lazy and submit to forced labor.

Dan's tribe would be treacherous.

Gad would be vulnerable to raids and invasions.

Asher's tribe would be prosperous farmers.

Naphtali would be a free spirit.

Benjamin's tribe became known for their warlike nature – even causing a civil war among the twelve tribes. Israel's first king, Saul, is from this tribe, as well as the Apostle Paul in the New Testament.

Joseph's descendants would be fruitful and expansive. Joseph's two sons, Ephraim and Manasseh, each got equal portions, the same as their uncles, the other sons of Jacob.

Benjamin and Judah together became known as the southern tribe of Judah.

The other ten tribes were the northern tribes of Israel. These ten tribes were later dispersed through the lands and are sometimes called the "lost" tribes of Israel.

The tribe of Judah was taken away from their lands and later returned.

From this description only the tribe of Judah would provide leadership and be successful for a long time. However, some of the great leaders of the Old Testament came from the line of Levi. Moses and Aaron were Levites. The whole basis of the Exodus from Egypt and the Law of the Jews can be attributed to the actions and faith of Moses and Aaron. The prophesy Jacob made, in his blessing of Levi, was fulfilled when the tribe of Levite was chosen by God to be the priests in charge of the Ark of the Covenant. When the Promised Land was divided amongst the tribes, the tribe of Levi received no large territory of their own. Instead they were dispersed to, and given, several towns throughout the land. The prophets of the Old Testament were probably also members of the Levi tribe.

The tribe of Judah begot the line of David. Almost everyone reading this knows from Bible stories about the young David slaying the giant. King David brought the twelve tribes together into a peaceful, unified, and centralized government at Jerusalem. A long line of kings descended from David until the dynasty was dispersed by foreign invaders.

In the New Testament, John The Baptizer was also a member of the Levite tribe. This is significant because this ties the priesthood of the Old Testament to the New Testament Savior, Jesus Christ. John The Baptizer performed the water baptism of Jesus Christ and witnessed the Spirit of God coming upon Jesus. At that point, the job of the Levite tribe was finished. Mary, the human mother of Jesus, had married Joseph who was a member of the tribe of Judah and a descendant of King David. *The line of David was fulfilled in the birth of Jesus Christ.*

Section Two:

Understanding the Bible

Edward F. LeGault

Chapter Six
Translations vs. Versions

Way back, when I was in school, I remember writing those book reports we all had to do. In Elementary school, they were fairly easy… they were nothing more than a short recap of the story. By high school and then later in college we had to write more about the intentions of the authors, and their hidden messages and meanings. There were stories like *Of Mice and Men*, *Romeo and Juliet*, *Lord of the Flies*, *The Chronicles of Narnia*, and *The Lord of the Rings*. Most authors will deny the meanings which others see in their works. For example, even though J.R.R Tolkien and C.S. Lewis admitted getting into some great discussions about life, philosophy and religion at Oxford, both of them often denied writing any special religious or spiritual meanings into many of their popular fictional works.

So, now we come to the epic work known as the Bible. When I started studying the Bible, one of the first problems I encountered were all the different "versions" of the Bible: *King James Version* (KJV), the *New King James Version* (NKJV), *American Standard Version* (ASV), *New American*

Edward F. LeGault

Standard Version (NASV), the *New International Version* (NIV), etc. Now you can add some more, such as the *NET Bible* and the *WEB Bible*. One of the biggest arguments anti-Christians (atheists, etc) try to use against a Christian is that there are all of these different "versions" of the Bible out there, and if there was really a God, and the Bible was the Word of God, then there would be only one Bible.

But, it is not that there are a bunch of different versions as much as there are different *translations*. Pick up a copy of the King James Bible. This was the translation from ancient Greek, Aramaic and Hebrew to the common language spoken at the time of the translation in the year 1611. That work may have been the very last translation by scholars who actually spoke, read and wrote ancient Greek as easily as they did their native language. So, although there are errors in the translation (I'll go into that in just a bit), it does give us a good look at translating ancient language texts into Olde English. And there lies one of the problems with current use of the King James Version. No one I know goes about speaking with "thee" and "thou" in their daily life outside of a Shakespeare class, play, or maybe at a Renaissance Faire.

So the first problem in reading and studying the Bible is getting a text which reads in the language of our current society and culture. The second problem is that there have been many different archeological finds giving us more actual copies or parts of very early Scripture writings. Most people have heard of the Dead Sea Scrolls. These scroll fragments give a much later look at early Old Testament writings than were available to the earlier translations of the Bible (such as the KJV). And, there have been many subsequent archeological findings since. These have all been studied by language and theology experts in recent years to give us more accurate and complete translations of the ancient, more original Biblical texts.

What I want to look for in a translation (aka "version") of the Bible is one which uses as much of the known available archeological text and writings as possible, translates into my current language used by my culture, AND *stays true to our Christian Biblical principles*. It is all right to fix mistakes in previous translations, but it is not all right to change such important tenants of the Bible as God being the Father, and for Christians the basic New Testament foundation of Jesus being the Son of God, along with the Holy Spirit rounding out the Holy Triune.

When reading and studying the Bible, there are a whole lot of things to consider. These will be some of the ideas shown in the following chapters.

Edward F. LeGault

Chapter Seven
Problems with Translations

Have you ever picked up a textbook, started reading it and did
not understand it? This happens all the time with college-
level courses in sciences, engineering, finance and many other
subjects. The authors obviously are experts in their area of
study or teaching, and their peers probably understand the
meanings of the subjects. If the textbook explains the new
subjects clearly to students, then the textbook writers have
done their job. Now pick up a non-fiction history book
centered on medieval Europe. Some of the culture and
customs are familiar, and some are not unless you are a
student of that era. Even the language is different. My wife
and daughter are renaissance faire fans. They dress up in that
era clothing and speak that Olde English. When I go with
them to a renaissance fair I have them to translate and explain
to me what is happening or what something means.

But, now take an ancient text, written in an original language,
which you don't know how to read, written in an era in which
you don't understand the customs and the culture, and now
you can have a difficult time understanding what the strange

Edward F. LeGault

words say. Never mind understanding what they mean in comparison to today's society.

If we were looking at a different type of a text, such as one of the works of Shakespeare, we would want to get to know the history of the author, the common culture at the time of the writings and the political happenings around the time of Shakespeare's life. We can do a similar investigative study of the Bible to gain a foundation of its history.

Chapter Eight
The Old Testament's Roots

The Jewish Torah is very similar to the Christian Old
Testament. This is not surprising since the roots of
Christianity can be found in its Judeo background. Jesus and
most of his original followers were Jewish, or Israelites.

The original stories of the Old Testament were handed down
from generation to generation verbally until a written
language, writing implements and methods of recording on a
somewhat permanent media were invented. There were no
printing presses. The writings were recorded on animal skins.
Professional scribes were used to copy one animal skin scroll
to another, character by character, line by line, paragraph by
paragraph, and document by document. Imperfect copies were
destroyed or buried. (Note: some of these "imperfect" copies
are what are often today found buried in archelogical sites.)

These various documents making up the Old Testament, or
Torah, were gathered together to make a complete text.
Somehow, somewhere, someone had to decide what was
included and what was not. This is the notion of a "canon". It

is not the modern brand of a camera or the historical projectile weapon of pirates and the civil war.

Canon means a collection of religious writings divinely inspired and hence authoritative, normative, sacred, and binding. The origin of the word canon is from the Hebrew word, *qaneh*, meaning a reed or measuring rod.

The Jews divided what we call the Old Testament into three classes of writings: the Law, the Prophets, and the Writings or Hagiographa. The Jews group the Old Testament books into 22, 24 or 27 books, depending on which authority and time period is taken into account for the groupings of the same writings into books. The earliest version of the Old Testament was the *Septuagint Version* (circa 250 -150 B.C.)

The Protestant Bible typically breaks some of the same writings into smaller books, such as 1 and 2 Kings, 1 and 2 Chronicles, 1 and 2 Samuel, the Minor Prophets into individual books, etc. The Roman Catholics add some of the apocryphal books to their Bibles to get 7 extra books for a total of 46 OT books. The Christian Old Testament was first translated into Greek, then Latin and then into German, etc.

Versions are based on the written language used and the particular canon authorities.

The four sources, or focal points, of authority for early Christianity was the prior position of the Jewish Old Testament canon, the "Word of the Lord", the place of the Holy Spirit, and the authoritative position of the apostles. These will be covered more in the section on understanding Christianity.

Chapter Nine
The New Testament's Roots

The New Testament, of course, was written after the life of
Jesus. We can divide the written works of the New Testament
into some categories:

- Those written by his personal friends and disciples
  (Matthew, Mark and John);
- Those written by an investigator (Luke);
- The letters of a post-crucifixion witness (Paul);
- And the letters to or from some of the other witnesses
  or disciples of Jesus.

Many of the letters, or epistles, are collections from the
Apostle Paul. The two theories concerning the collection of
Paul's epistles are:

(1) The early churches exchanged and shared the writings, or
(2) some individual took it upon himself to collect copies of
all of Paul's letters.

Remember, there were no modern conveniences such as we

Edward F. LeGault

have now for communications and the recording of events. Letters from an important church leader was not only cherished, but also copied (by scribes) and sent on to other church centers.

Then, they were gathered into collections. But, somebody had to decide which were "holy", or "God divined", and which were not divine writings. Some of the early church leaders in the development of the Christian Bible canon from A.D. 140-180 were Marcion of Sinope, Montanus, Justin Martyr, Melito of Sardis, Athenagoras of Athens, and the Scillitan Martyrs. There were no doubt disputes among those very early theologians about deciding which writings would be included in the Bible.

The Muratorian Fragment is a list of Biblical books, written in barbarous Latin, discovered by the Italian historian Muratori in 1740. The Muratorian Fragment is important because it contains a list of apostolic books "for the whole Church" which can be read in public in the Church. It also gives details concerning the author, destination, occasion, and purpose of the books listed therein.

Then, in A.D. 367, the Alexandrian theologian, Athanasius wrote the thirty-ninth Easter letter listing the 27 books of the present New Testament canon and declaring them to be a canonical collection to which nothing is to be taken away nor added.

Some passages in the New Testament cover the importance of that text:

- The text of 2 Tim 3:16 is Paul's assertion of the divine origin of Scripture: *Every Scripture is God-breathed (inspired by God) and profitable for teaching, for reproof, for correction, and for instruction in righteousness...*

- The text of 2 Peter 1:19-21 has Peter offering his readers the testimony of eyewitnesses of Christ's glory: *We have the more sure word of prophecy; and you do well that you heed it, as to a lamp shining in a dark place, until the day dawns, and the morning star arises in your hearts; knowing this first, that no prophecy of Scripture is of private interpretation. For no prophecy ever came by the will of man: but holy men of God spoke, being moved by the Holy Spirit.*

- And finally, the main point of John 10:34-36 is the legal authority of the **entire** Scripture, not just the OT Law: *Jesus answered them, "Isn't it written in your law, 'I said, you are gods? If he called them gods, to whom the word of God came (and the Scripture can't be broken), do you say of him whom the Father sanctified and sent into the world, 'You blaspheme,' because I said, 'I am the Son of God?"* (Jesus was both the expert on God's Word and the fulfillment of God's Word.)

Now we have an Old Testament and a New Testament to read and study. How do we go about that?

Edward F. LeGault

Chapter Ten
Translating the Bible

Hermeneutics, as used here, is the study of the theory and practice of interpretation of the Bible: the task of discovering what the meaning is in today's language and culture. One of the problems with interpreting an ancient text is trying to understand not only what the text meant (back then), but also what it means (today). In an ideal world the meaning would be the same.

The aim of good interpretation is to have a balance between what was meant in the original language by the original writer and what it means to the reader here and now. Two facts that become a challenge as we face the need to interpret scripture are:

(1) the Word was originally given in a specific concrete historical context, and
(2) the need to understand what the Living Word means to us today in our different culture and language.

We start by understanding the ancient culture, society and

language. **Exegesis** is the task to find out what the text originally meant in the original writer's language and culture.

There are three different theories of translation:

- *Literal* translation, i.e., the attempt to translate as close from the original language through a <u>word by word</u> translation to a modern language.
- *Free* translation, i.e., the attempt to translate <u>ideas</u> from the original language to a modern language without regard to exact word translations (a paraphrase).
- *Dynamic equivalent* translation, i.e., the attempt to translate original words, idioms, and grammatical constructions into <u>precise equivalents</u> in the receptor language.

Euphemisms are words or expressions substituted for others which are culturally offensive to good manners. The translation of euphemisms can subtly change the meaning of words and expressions.

Translators have the option of translating ancient texts:

- Literally to a bewildering meaning;
- Translate to an offensive literal equivalent;
- Or translate to a culturally equivalent euphemism.

There is a very real danger of the translator missing the meaning of the original idiom. Grammar and syntax are a problem in translation because each language has its own unique preferred structure and word relationships. Direct or literal translations become awkward reading. Dynamic equivalent translations depend on the translators having a good working knowledge of the original manuscript language and meanings in context of the writer's history, culture and geography.

The areas of time, culture, customs and language affect our ability to interpret early Biblical texts. We don't truly understand what it was like to live in the first century world (at the time of Jesus). Our understanding of the early New Testament manuscripts is hindered by the differences between life then and now.

Edward F. LeGault

Chapter Eleven
Interpreting the Bible

The *goal* of interpretation is application of Biblical concepts to our daily lives. **Interpretation** is the *technique of understanding* the meaning of God's Word.

(**Application** is figuring out *how to use* the new found information, or concepts, in our daily lives).

Following are the four principles for observing what is actually found in the Bible:

- Beware of *preconceived* ideas. Observe what the text actually says. Forget any legends or sayings improperly attributed to the Bible.

- Read or observe the text first, in context of the text before and after, then explain it. *Ensure the explanation fits the observation and not vice versa.*

- Do not rely on preferred theology beliefs before shaping your own explanation based on your observations.

- Consider the importance of any details noticed in the observation.

-- *Essential* details are *necessary* to the story line.
-- *Accidental* details are *not important* to the story.

Read the text with and without the selected details. If the meaning is clear without the detail, then it is <u>accidental</u> in nature. If the meaning changes or is unknown without the detail, then it is <u>essential</u> to the story.

Literary context is the words, sentences, paragraphs, or chapters that surround and relate to a text. It is the surrounding text from which a particular word, phrase, sentence, or paragraph is plucked. This is important for a better understanding of any particular text.

Historical context is the culture, customs, languages, beliefs and history of the author and his original audience. It is the time and place where the original text was set.

Traditions bring commitments and preconceptions to our thinking. This leads us to make *premature* judgments about things before we have had time to finish our observations and make our own interpretations based on the text alone.

Textual criticism is a science that works with careful controls by using both external evidence, i.e., the character and quality of old manuscripts, and internal evidence reflected by the quality of the actual authors or copyists (scribes). Textual criticism is not an exact science because it deals with too many human variables.

We should be aware of the following three concerns, or problems, about *textual criticism*:

- There are no original manuscripts of the Bible in existence today.

- There are thousands of copies produced by hand over a period of 1400 years.

- Although the later copies from the late medieval period are much alike, they differ significantly from earlier copies.

The role of *theology* is to use the wisdom of the scholars who came before us to prevent our misinterpreting scripture. Since most of us are not theology experts, what can we do to help us understand the original writers of the Biblical texts?

Some of the goals of the study of historical context enable us to grasp a bigger picture of the Biblical writings:

- *Who* was the writer?

- *Who* was it written to?

- *When* was it written?

- *Where* was it written?

- *Why* was it written?

- *What* were the customs and politics when it was written?

We can learn about antiquity (ancient customs and cultures) by using background information found in scripture passages, sermons, and Bible study notes. We can also use Bible encyclopedias, dictionaries and other study aids to learn about the particular time period.

The relationship between the ancient author and the reader sets the tone and underlying substance of the writing. If the reader was expected to be accepting of the writings, then the work is written expecting the readers to accept the message without reservation.

If the tone of the writings was a rebuke, then the author expected there to be tension between himself and the reader, perhaps even rejection of the message. In the ambivalent relationship, the reader knows what the text is and respects it, but goes ahead and ignores the Truth in the writings.

Interpreting a passage of text can be done by small steps or stages:

- Interpret single verses in context of the verses immediately surrounding them.

- Interpret paragraphs or events in the context of the surrounding paragraphs or events.

- Assume all scripture is written by men, but inspired by God.

- Try to determine why God placed a particular section of text where it is... and not some other place in the Bible.

- Look for themes that open or close a particular section of text.

- Look for word or phrases that are repeated throughout the section of text.

- Determine the purpose of the text in its section and book.

- If a stated purpose can be found written by the original author then it should be used; otherwise try to formulate your own.

- Reports or records of events should be compared to other reports or records of events to discover the themes.

- In speech stories, what is said is more important than the story surrounding it.

- The main point of the story is usually revealed through the resolution of a conflict.

- To make a proper application of a biblical narrative we must explore repeated ideas or words. Also, very few details are usually given and we must explore those which are given... and carefully fill in the blanks.

In school, students are tasked with interpreting various stories or books. A story plot is usually a drama consisting of different stages, episodes or sections of the story. We can use similar techniques to analyze stories and events in the Bible.

Edward F. LeGault

The aspects of a biblical drama are as follows:

- Setting the stage involves looking at the time (short or long), the spatial setting (inside or outside, at home or at war, in a town setting or a holy place, etc.), and the social setting (meals, sabbath, holidays, etc.).

- Understanding the characters in the Biblical drama includes looking at both individuals and groups. There are typically believers, unbelievers, and undecided characters. The characters will probably have different traits, thoughts, and deeds.

- A Biblical drama usually has at least one type of conflict such as a test, a quest, or a choice.

- Obstacles mount through conflict until the climax of the story.

- The resolution of the conflict leads to the principle being taught.

- The follow-up action or saying interprets the biblical drama.

Discourse analysis is the study of the way authors put their story together with sentences and paragraphs to make their points.

Look for clues that are spread out through a particular text passage or story:

- What is the location of the main idea or theme (i.e., the first or the last sentence)?

- Does the writer repeat, or restate, the main concept?

- Does the writer address the reader before stating a main idea?

- Does the writer draw attention with an introductory formula such as "I want you to know..." or "I am writing these things..."

- Does the writer use concluding formulas such as "therefore", "thus" or "so"?

We can put together some of what we have learned by analyzing and interpreting the following passage (Romans 12:1):

Therefore, I urge you, brothers, by the mercies of God, to present your bodies a living sacrifice, holy, acceptable to God, which is your spiritual service.

Therefore = this is a concluding passage of something said earlier.
I urge you = the introduction.
brothers = who is being addressed (familiar persons).
to present your bodies = this is the main thought.
to God = the object of the main thought.

But, the process of interpretation of the Bible is not always easy or without problems. Some of these problems are outlined below.

Edward F. LeGault

1. <u>Obvious problems</u>. These include things such as names of people and places, customs, or other words about which we know little or nothing. An example would be found in Matthew 8:8 below:

The centurion answered, "Lord, I'm not worthy for you to come under my roof..."

What is a *centurion*? Is this someone that is 100 years old? No, it is a captain in the Roman army of 100 soldiers.

2. <u>Teacher problems</u>. Teachers, leaders, and pastors should not assume all listeners or participants have the same knowledge level. This can be experienced in many Bible studies or church sermons. Does everyone in the audience know the meaning of words such as *redemption, revelation, prophesy,* etc.?

3. <u>Hidden problems</u>. These problems occur when we encounter words or phrases which we think we know, but on closer examination we realize there are deeper meanings. Some of this will have to do with local customs and translations. The English language has the word "love." Other languages, such as Greek or Hebrew, may have several different words for the whole range of meanings in the English language.

For example:

> I *love* my wife.
> I *love* my child.
> I *love* my job.
> I *love* my dog.

These four cases of the use of the word "love" all have different meanings. Other languages could have four (or more) separate words to translate to our word, "love".

Solutions to these three problems can be found by using good reference materials such as Bible dictionaries and encyclopedias. Those type of books will help us understand the customs, places and people that are new to us.

Studying particular *themes* is very popular in many Bible studies, but this can tend to limit our understanding of God's word. God gave us a whole book of principles for study. If we only have thematic studies we limit ourselves to only certain scriptures <u>pulled out of context</u> as they relate to the specified theme. **Scripture needs to be studied in the whole context of the chapter, book, or set of books**, of the Bible from which it is plucked.

I know this is contradictory, but thematic studies are very popular amongst pastors and churches. If you must be involved in a thematic study, here are the steps to follow in order to develop a thematic study:

- Begin with one central text for a theme, then expand to others throughout the Bible.

- It is vital to differentiate between the concept being studied and the individual words of that concept. For example, when studying the consequences of a person becoming a believer, in Matthew 10:34 we find, *"Don't think that I came to send peace on the earth. I didn't come to send peace, but a sword."* If we concentrate a study on the word, "sword", we will get side-tracked from the idea of a family relationship that is divided by non-believers and believers.

- Ask more questions of peers, pastors and Bible study leaders, and then brainstorm.

- Use several cross references to find other related passages.

- Scan a Bible concordance, but be aware that word studies themselves can be possibly counter-productive.

- Read a Bible dictionary and a Bible encyclopedia article on the subject in question.

- Consult a handbook of systematic or Biblical theology.

- Learn the times and culture through reading and researching Bible dictionaries, encyclopedias, or other reference material. (Note: In this time of the Internet, be careful of "wiki" references or other "Biblical" articles and websites… they can be literally written by **anyone**, whether they are a credentialed expert or not!).

- Ensure that the theme of the passage fits the overall theme of the paragraph, chapter, book, and set of books if necessary.

- Know how to find the theme in the story by looking at the first or last sentence, or the climax of the story.

- Notice if and where words, phrases, or ideas are repeated.

- Study and listen to the dialog found in the narrative,

drama, etc.

- Look for exaggerated or unusual details. Try to figure out what the author was trying to show you or prove to you.

- Observe quotations or allusions to other scripture that might give a hint from the author.

- Look for *irony* to discover the opposite of the most apparent meaning in the story.

Our quest for understanding of ancient cultures is important to the process of problem solving because the *original setting* of the writings will have an effect on gaining an understanding of the original intent. The whole scope of the language translation will be dependent on knowing the *nuances* of the intent of the original writer. Understanding the culture, geography, political situations, etc., will help us to understand the original point.

The Word of God on the divine level is always based on God's Truth. The human level is man's need to understand how the Word of God applies to him at a particular time and place in history. Fortunately the Truth is always out there in scripture as a Living Word.

Edward F. LeGault

Chapter Twelve
Applying Scripture

The next stage after learning to *interpret* God's Word from
Biblical scripture is to utilize **what** you have learned to apply
to <u>your everyday life</u>.

Application is figuring out *how to use* the new found
information or concepts in our daily lives.

Two critical elements for the process of application of Biblical
scripture in our lives are:

- A solid knowledge and practice of exegesis.

- An understanding of our culture today.

We must proceed in these steps to achieve a proper
application of Biblical text:

- We must determine the original meaning of the text.

- We must find the principle behind the text.

Edward F. LeGault

- Then apply the principle to a similar situation today.

- If possible, verify your conclusions by comparing them to other Scriptures.

More specifically we learn:

- Laws or rules require obedience to specific commands.

- Ideals or principles guide a wide range of behavior without specifying particular deeds.

- Actions in narratives depict positive examples to be imitated, and negative examples to be avoided.

- Biblical symbols and images create new ways of seeing things.

- Doctrines are cardinal beliefs of the faith and convictions.

- Divine promises are commitments by God.

- Songs and prayers found in Biblical scripture show us how to worship and pray.

But, we need to be very careful when learning to utilize the application of Biblical Scripture:

- Who applies scripture? Is it applied by God, the teacher, the student, or the reader?

- How does the application take place? Does the

application occur by some workings of the Holy Spirit, or by our own hard work and soul searching?

- What is the purpose or goal of the application? Is the goal personal or is it for the greater community good? Is the goal of the application better fellowship with God or for greater human happiness?

These problems directly relate to the *authority* of Scripture. If we try to deny that the Truths of our Holy Scripture are as valid today as they were thousands of years ago, then we have a problem with an all-knowing, all-present, all-powerful God. We should first concentrate on discovering the Truth and authority of God from scripture, then apply the Truth to our lives today.

Some more approaches to scriptural application are:

- Let the scriptural application flow from our own *personal spirituality* and *meditation*. This is subjective and based on one's own experiences learned in the school of life. One drawback of this approach is that relying on meditation allows us to hear **other** voices aside from just the Lord's.

- Another approach to scriptural application is to *let God do it* by having a direct encounter with Him. This approach relies on the inherent capacity of God to touch our lives by preparing us to listen to His word.

- *Hard work* based on training on exegesis and development of a good moral character. A teacher must be ready for both reluctant listeners looking for spiritual entertainment **and** eager learners who will have many

Edward F. LeGault

follow-up questions. This type of application calls for both perseverance in study and also the imagination to connect ideas in unexpected ways.

- A *passive* involvement letting your slowly increasing knowledge and spirituality lead you down the right path. This can be a dangerous endeavor if one is not surrounded by a good support group and mentors.

- *Reflection* is a method, or technique, to discover and teach the main lesson of Biblical texts through a series of steps or questions to discover the topic of the text, what the passage teaches about the topic, and how the main point applies to the audience.

In summary, to be strong in the art of bible scripture application one needs to be of a good moral character, be willing to listen to God, work hard in studying scripture, and have a good imagination… in order to be ready to connect ideas in an appropriate manner.

Section III:

Understanding Christianity

Edward F. LeGault

Chapter Thirteen
What Christians Believe

About God: God is the Creator and Ruler of the universe. He eternally exits in three personalities: the Father, the Son, and the Holy Spirit. These three are co-equal and are **one** God.

Genesis 1:1, 26-27, 3:22
Psalm 90:2
Matthew 28:19
1 Peter 1:2
2 Corinthians 13:14

About Jesus: Jesus Christ is the Son of God. He is co-equal with the Father. Jesus lived a sinless human life and offered Himself as the perfect sacrifice for the sins of all people by dying on a cross. He arose from the dead after three days to demonstrate His power over sin and death. He ascended to Heaven's glory and will return again someday as King of Kings and Lord of Lords.

Matthew 1:22-23

Edward F. LeGault

Isaiah 9:6
John 1:1-5, 14:10-30
Hebrews 4:14, 15
1 Corinthians 15:3-4
Romans 1:3-4
Acts 1:9-11
1 Timothy 6:14-15
Titus 2:13

About the Holy Spirit: The Holy Spirit is co-equal with the Father and the Son of God. He is present in the world to make men and women aware of their need for Jesus Christ. He also lives in every Christian from the moment of salvation. He provides the Christian with power for living, understanding of spiritual truth, and guidance in doing what is right. He gives every believer a spiritual gift when they are saved. As Christians, we seek to live under His control daily.

2 Corinthians 3:17
John 16:7-13, 14:16-17
Acts 1:18
1 Corinthians 2:12, 3:16
Ephesians 1:13
Galatians 5:25
Ephesians 5:18

About the Bible: The Bible is God's Word to us. It was written by human authors under the supernatural guidance of the Holy Spirit. It is the supreme source of Truth for Christian beliefs and Christian living. Because it is inspired by God, it is the Truth without any mixture of error.

2 Timothy 3:16

2 Peter 1:20-21
2 Timothy 1:13
Psalm 119:105,160, 12:6
Proverbs 30:5

About Salvation: People are made in the spiritual image of God, to be like Him in character. People are the supreme object of God's creation. Although every person has tremendous potential for good, all of us are marred by an attitude of disobedience toward God, known as *sin.* This attitude, or sin, separates people from God and causes many problems in our lives.

Genesis 1:27
Psalm 8:3-6
Isaiah 53:6a
Romans 3:23
Isaiah 59:1-2

About Eternity: People were created to exist forever. We will either exist eternally separated **from** God by sin, or eternally **with** God through forgiveness and salvation. To be eternally separated from God is Hell. To be eternally in union with Him is eternal life. Heaven and Hell are real places of eternal existence.

John 3:16
John 14:17
Romans 6:23
Romans 8:17-18
Revelation 20:15
1 Corinthians 2:7-9

Edward F. LeGault

In essential beliefs – we have unity.

"There is one Body and one Spirit... there is one Lord, one faith, one baptism, and one God and Father of us all..."
Ephesians 4:4-6

In non-essential beliefs – we have liberty.

"Accept him whose faith is weak, without passing judgment on disputable matters... Who are you to judge someone else's servant? To his own master he stands or fails... So then each of us will give you an account of himself to God... So whatever you believe about these things keep between yourself and God."
Romans 14:1,4,12,22

In all our beliefs – we show charity.

"... If I hold in my mind not only all human knowledge but also the very secrets of God, and if I have the faith that can move mountains – but have no love, I amount to nothing at all."
1 Corinthians 13:2

Chapter 14
Atonement

You may have seen the signs or banners at sporting events. Or even inscribed on hats and other clothing. Sometimes even on peoples' heads or tattooed on bodies: "**John 3:16**". It is probably the most quoted Bible verse in the world.

What is it, and what does it mean?

"For God so loved the world, that he gave his one and only Son, that whoever believes in him should not perish, but have eternal life."
- John 3:16

Noah Webster defined *atonement* as "…(an) agreement or reconciliation; expiation; satisfaction or reparation made by giving an equivalent for an injury, or by doing or suffering that which is received in satisfaction for an offense or injury."

Depending on the Bible translation, the word *atonement* is mentioned about one hundred times in the Old Testament. The same word is only mentioned about three times in the New

Testament. The majority of the Old Testament occurrences are in the book of Leviticus, where the various Jewish Laws are given to the Israelites.

The Hebrew word *kapar*, translated to our English verb to *atone*, means to *cover over, atone, propitiate, or pacify*. This verb is first used in the Old Testament account in Genesis 6:14 of God telling Noah to cover over the ark with pitch. The Hebrew noun *kapporet* is translated to mean *mercy seat* or *throne of mercy* (1 Chron 28:11), referring to the slab of gold resting on top of the Ark of the Covenant. This mercy seat, or throne of God, symbolized His presence in the temple back room. The Hebrew word *kaphar*, meaning to *cover* or to *cancel*, is translated as *atonement*. The Greek word *katallage* is translated as *atonement* but actually means *reconciliation* as used in Rom 5:11 or 2 Cor 5:18.

In Old Testament history, the method of choice for obtaining atonement was by presenting offerings and sacrifices to God. This act of bringing offerings for sacrifice was conducted in order to bring a gift to God in an attempt to buy His favor. There were several categories of offerings, such as a *voluntary offering* to be burnt partially on the alter and then the remainder consumed by the priests and Israelites, the *tithe* of livestock and grains which were sold by the temple priests for money or consumed for food, and the *required offering* which was to be burnt wholly on the alter.

The animal offerings used for the sacrificial ceremonies were an attempt by the Jews to atone, or cover over, the Israelite's sin. The shedding of blood was an integral part of the paying the price, or atoning, for one's sin. Leviticus 17:11 tells us God said, "*For the life of a creature is in the blood, and I have given it to you to make atonement for yourselves on the altar; it is the blood that makes atonement for one's life.*"

The Jewish people had a particular annual rite of atonement. The Day of Atonement, or Yom Kippur, itself was set aside for the ritualistic cleansings of the temple building, alter and sanctuary. This provided a clean meeting place for God to be with His people. The cleansing, or atonement, of inanimate objects was restricted to the temple building itself and the inner sanctum where the Ark resided. Otherwise, the sacrificial atonement processes were for the chosen people of God, the Israelites [Evangelical Dictionary of Theology].

An interesting bit of theology is that God let the Israelites substitute animal blood sacrifices for payment of *human* sins. The animal had to have been a male and blemish free -- as perfect as possible, but still an animal other than a human being. Whereas a few pagan idol worshipers may have tried an occasional human blood sacrifice, we know from Gen 22:12, when God provided the animal sacrifice during the testing of Abraham, that God did **not** approve of humans providing other humans to be sacrificed for others' atonement. The only way God could approve a human sacrifice was for Him to provide it Himself (via his Son's death).

John, the Baptizer, preceded Jesus by preparing the way for the eventual baptism of Jesus Christ and His (Jesus') subsequent receipt of the Holy Spirit. John the Baptizer's earlier work was one of baptizing for repentance, through the simple ritual of full body immersion in water. This simple *symbolic* ritual probably replaced the complicated ceremonial washings which the Old Testament era Israelites had been doing as part of their sacrificial atonement rituals. The Old Testament sacrifices, which had covered-over the sins of men with animal blood, had now temporarily been replaced with the participants' expressing their desire for forgiveness through water immersion baptism.

John, the Baptizer, upon seeing Jesus in His first public Godly manifestation, declared, as recorded in John 1:29, "*Behold the Lamb of God, which taketh away the sin of the world.*" John, the Baptizer, had obviously been given special insight by God about Jesus, who was the perfect, ultimate and **final** sacrificial element for the atonement of the sins of **all** mankind.

Whereas atonement in the Old Testament history had been attempted through sacrifices offered to God by man, **true salvation or redemption was given to mankind by God through the sacrificial gift of His Son, Jesus Christ, on the cross.** The importance of redemption is because this life on Earth is temporary. Eternal life, after death, will either be *with* God or *separated* from God. Redemption, through God's grace, guarantees eternal life *with* God. The alternative, of *separation* from God, is not good and results in damnation to hell and final destruction in a pit of fire, along with Satan.

In the book of Acts, chapter 22, we read about Paul (formerly Saul) after his encounter with Jesus on the road to Damascus. He is visited by a man named Ananias, who tells him in verse 16, "*...be baptized and wash away your sins, calling on His name.*"

Our Lord God has taken thousands of years to lead His people to the only true Way of redemption, i.e., through the punishment and blood sacrifice of His own Son to wash away the sins of all of us who accept Jesus Christ as our Savior and redeemer. Jesus, the Son of God, was made man, born of a woman, to walk the earth as the *only* sinless person, to be sacrificed for the atonement of **our** sins.

Chapter 15
Who is this Jesus?

One of the principles of Christianity is the concept of the
Trinity, or three heads or parts, of God: The Father, the Son,
and the Holy Spirit. A most difficult concept to grasp is the
concept of God being born man in the form of Jesus Christ.
Jesus was born unto a woman (Mary, who was engaged to
Joseph of Nazareth) who was a virgin (had not had any sexual
relations).

Jesus was both God and man. He was born into this world, but
He was without sin (he had to be sin-less because He was
God). He grew up, learned to be a carpenter from his step-
father, Joseph, and started his ministry work somewhere
around the age of 33. His work is full of miracles and
teachings. The early life of Jesus is not the object of this book.
However, we will touch on some of his teaching life.

In chapter 6 of the Gospel of John, we can read about Jesus
feeding the five thousand followers with five small barley
loaves and two small fish brought by a young boy (John 6:5-
13). After this miracle had occurred, the masses of people

wanted to *forcibly* crown Jesus as their king. Since this was not in God's plan, Jesus withdrew to a mountain (vv 14-15).

Jesus later meets his disciples on the stormy water (vv 16-21). In verses 32-40 Jesus told the crowd that it was not Moses that gave their ancestors manna from heaven, but it was God, the Father. Then Jesus gave them the new concept of "*For the bread of God is He who comes down from Heaven and gives life to the world*" (v 33).

In verses 51-58 of chapter 6 of the Gospel of John, Jesus proclaims "*I am the living bread that came down from heaven. If anyone eats of this bread, he will live forever. This bread is my flesh, which I will give for the life of the world*" (v 51), "*...I tell you the truth, unless you eat the flesh of the Son of Man and drink his blood, you have no life in you. Whoever eats my flesh and drinks my blood has eternal life, and I will raise him up at the last day*" (v 53-54), and "*This is the bread that came down from heaven. Your forefathers ate manna and died, but he who feeds on this bread will live forever*" (v 58).

Jesus has repeatedly used symbolism for His explanations of His divine heritage and lineage. Sometimes the listeners might have understood His metaphors and symbols, but this time many of the listeners were disturbed by Jesus' apparent reference to His flesh and His blood.

In Old Testament times, blood sacrifices were a common part of both the Israelites and pagan idol worshiper's cultures. Animal blood and human blood were both linked to the very meaning of life (Vine's). The high value of life itself, as a gift from God, led to the Jewish prohibition against the eating or drinking of blood (Gen 9:4, Lev 3:17, Lev 7:26).

The thought of actually eating flesh and drinking blood must have been repugnant to those followers who had not listened well to Jesus. Like many people, even people in these current times, as soon as they heard something that seemed to contradict their pre-conceived ideas or customs, they ran away from the Good News (John 6:66).

[Members of Christian churches should be sensitive to visitors, seekers and new members at their churches when selecting songs, worship themes and sermon messages. The message of blood, sacrifices and death, although a true part of Christianity, can be frightening to the unknowing newcomer].

Jesus was trying to make these points:

- If God was faithful and provided temporary subsistence through His daily gift of manna to their ancestors, then surely God could provide eternal life through the sacrificial gift of His own Son.

- He (Jesus) had made many references to His Father, thereby equating Himself with God the Father.

- Jesus had performed many miracles. But, many interested followers had missed His point that He, **Jesus**, fulfilled the Old Testament prophesies concerning the coming Messiah.

And, they (the Jews) also missed the main point that God was ready to complete His plan. God had proven that His people could never gain redemption on their own: just read the Old Testament. Now, only through faith in Jesus, could they gain atonement worthy of Eternal Life with God in Heaven (John 6:36-40).

Edward F. LeGault

Chapter 16
Faith

In today's world we must remember to put our complete faith in Jesus Christ. We have the advantage of all of God's Word having been released to us through His scripture.

We can read and study all of it, but *we must **not** lose sight of the basics of God's eternal plan*:

- we have a sinful nature,
- we are not capable of atonement of those sins by ourselves and,
- God sent His only Son to pay for **our** sins so that we can obtain *everlasting eternal life* with Him.

When dealing with church seekers and new Christians, it is important not to overload them with some of our Biblical and Christian language that might offend or frighten them away due to their limited knowledge or understanding, i.e., language such as the *blood of the lamb*, *drink my blood*, etc.

We need to be known as loving followers of Christ, who have

our faith placed in His redemption of our sins, and not as cannibals, vampires or weird sacrifice worshipers.

Chapter 3, of the Epistle to the Romans, begins with "*What advantage, then is there in being a Jew or what value is there in circumcision?*" This is a result of the end of chapter 2 (v 25-29) where Paul was writing about Jewish circumcision and the Law.

Is circumcision enough to keep a Jew right with God?
How about a Gentile who has not been circumcised?

Paul answers those questions as a reminder to his fellow Jews that *circumcision is only a **declaration** of one's intent on keeping the Law.* Circumcision itself is **not** the basis of righteousness or salvation.

Is not a Gentile who keeps the Law, but is not circumcised, not also a Jew?

Paul wrote that which differentiates the Jews from the Gentiles is not the Law and circumcision, but the covenant which God has made with the Jewish people.

Paul directs to the Jews their objections on his teachings with a series of questions and answers (Rom 3:1-8):

- *What is the advantage of being a Jew?* God entrusted The Jews with His Word and Truth, yet they repeatedly disregard Him.

- *What is the use of circumcision as a declaration of following God's if they are not going to do that (follow and obey God)?* God entrusted the Truths to the Jews over a long period of time. The Jews collected them and recorded them (truths, laws, commandments).

- *How did they respond with these?* Paul asserts that since the Jews disobeyed God through unfaithfulness then their *unfaithfulness* will not nullify God's faithfulness to His people. (He is always true.)

- *How, then, will God punish the unfaithful world?* If the Jews are repeatedly breaking the law and the Gentiles (the whole rest of the world) are not worthy, then what wrath must God bring on the world for punishment? God must condemn and punish the world for our sins. How will, or has, that been done?

What, then, are we to conclude? (Rom 3:9-20)?

- *Are the Jews better than the Gentiles?* No.

- *Are the Jews worse off than the Gentiles?* No.

- The better question should be, *"Do we have any guarantee to exclude us from God's wrath?"* We as sinners, Jew and Gentile alike, don't have what it takes to be perfect before God. We **need** help from God.

- Paul then makes a number of quotations from the Old Testament, especially from the book of Psalms. Sometimes the quotes are word for word, and sometimes he paraphrases for emphasis or simplicity. These verses deal with sin: the condition, attitude and conduct of the wicked in the heart.

- Paul returns to quotes from the Mosaic law to show the

failure of both the Jew and Gentile. *No one person deserves to be saved or acquitted of their sins.*

- Then, *what next?* God has been making His people aware of sin. Man can be something more than the sinful creature we have been since Adam & Eve.

The *righteousness of God* is **apart** from the Law (of the Israelites) (Rom 3:21-31).

Paul insists that faith, as righteousness, is not something new to the Old Testament Jew. *There is **no difference** between Jew and Gentile when it comes to sin.* All of us are very guilty. Adam's fall from Glory affects **all** men. *But the Glory of God can be seen and received by all men through Jesus Christ.* This Glory can be *freely received*, but **only by means of God's grace**.

God has provided a means of redemption that meets God's own strict requirements. **God has bought us back by paying the appropriate expensive price through His own son's death.** This blood sacrifice of His son was a necessary method of atoning for our sins, **but we must have faith in Jesus to receive the reward!**

God has provided us with a *faith-centered* system of redemption **replacing** the Old Testament's *works-centered* attempt for atonement.

Let me say that again: God has provided us with a *faith-centered* system of redemption **replacing** the Old Testament's *works-centered* attempt for atonement.

No more sacrifices, no more lists of godly works to complete.

Yes, loving Jesus Christ as your Lord and Savior should make your conscience *want* you to live a better life, but there is no checklist of works. DO NOT LET ANYONE CONVINCE YOU OTHERWISE!

I believe that not even baptism is necessary. Many Christians will argue otherwise, but that would then be a "works" and God's sacrifice of His only Son, Jesus, replaced ALL works. Baptism, since Jesus died and rose again, is now only a public display of one's having faith in Jesus as Lord and Savior. Baptism can be an important psychological, emotional and public display to your family, friends and community of a new commitment to Jesus and a change of life.

By God's Grace, all we have to do is to have faith in Jesus as our Lord and Savior… That's it… That is the big Christian "secret ingredient" to being saved from eternal hell and instead receiving eternal life with God. We still must pay for our sins, debts, trespasses, crimes, etc., in this life in the world. But, this is all temporary. Righteousness through faith, not through works, or sacrifices, rewards us with eternal life with God in the afterlife in a place known as Heaven.

Paul argues that righteousness through faith is not new (Rom 4:1-8). Paul looks at the life of Abraham, the father of the Jewish people. Paul quotes from Genesis 15:6 where God credited Abraham with righteousness because of his (Abraham's) belief and trust in the Lord. Paul then uses the analogy of work and wages: wages *are not a favor* to the worker, *but an obligation* to the employee by the employer for work done. Likewise, **he who has faith in the Lord must be credited with righteousness**.

This line of thought was likely to be unthinkable to some

Jewish people. The Jews have believed that thousands of years of tradition (of only following the Law) would get them right with God.

Paul is saying that *even the Godless and sinful could be redeemed*.

After all, Abraham was made father of all who believe before circumcision (Rom 4:9-12). Paul asserts Abraham had already been found to be a righteous man years before he was circumcised. The rite of circumcision was only meant to be a sign which confirms one's commitment to following God's laws. God had already made a promise, or covenant, that Abraham would be the father of a new nation... before Abraham was circumcised. Therefore **faith**, *not circumcision*, is what is necessary to be a righteous person.

Paul again asserts the promise for Abraham to be the father of the world was **not** through the law, *but through faith* (Rom 4:13-16). God bestows *righteousness on men through faith*. The law only produces God's wrath, because ***no one can keep the standards, that God has laid down, with the Jewish Law.***

God is the object of faith for both Abraham and the Christian (Rom 4:17-25). Paul reminds the reader of the obstacles which God overcame in the lives of Abraham and Sarah. Abraham was nearly 100 years old when God made His covenant for Abraham to be the father of the world. Sarah was too old to have children and had in fact been childless her entire life. Abraham had to fully trust God, for God had made a covenant (contract) with him. Paul reminds readers that **Abraham only knew God**, but *the Christian also knows of God raising up Christ for our redemption*.

Paul writes of the effects of the *righteousness by faith* upon the recipients (Rom 5:1-11). Peace and fellowship *are only accessible through Jesus Christ*. The testing of our faith through tribulation results in endurance and character building – and then hope brings the Glory of God through Jesus Christ. Now, *Jesus owns us* because of His payment for our sins. Therefore, we can be of one Spirit with Him.

*God **gives** us our reconciliation*, **we did not earn it**!

This is very important, let me say that again:
*God **gives** us our reconciliation (redemption)*, **we did not earn it**!

Paul finishes this section with a reminder of the effects of *Adam's disobedience* and *Christ's obedience* (Rom 5:12-21). **All** of us have sinned due to Adam's original sinful disobedience to God. *Adam's disobedience should have brought the wrath of God upon all men.* **But God had another plan**, i.e., the gift of righteousness bestowed on men by God through the **gift** of His son's death as our redemptive price. One man, Adam, caused a sinful mankind who should receive the full wrath of God. Instead, because of one man, Jesus Christ, **eternal death no longer will be the wrath for those sinners who believe in Jesus Christ through God's grace**.

Edward F. LeGault

Chapter 17
The Gospels

The word, *gospel*, is used to mean *the good news* (of Jesus Christ dying for our salvation). We commonly refer to the Gospels of the Apostles Matthew, Mark, Luke and John. Who were these men? Matthew, Mark and John were disciples, or students, of Jesus. Many thousands of people listened to the teachings of Jesus.

We know Jesus had a large group of seventy students, or disciples, of which twelve were in the "inner circle" with whom Jesus spent more time. Matthew, Mark and John were part of that group of twelve and were around Jesus during his ministry. I am sure some of them came and went as part of their own daily needs and the needs of the group. Some of them (the twelve) would have had to been off arranging housing and meals part of the time. Some probably worked part time to raise cash for their needs not met by donations of food and housing.

Luke, on the other hand, was **not** one of the original disciples of Jesus. He set out to investigate the life and death of Jesus (after the Crucifixion of Jesus) as a favor to a friend. His friend, Theophilus, was curious if the stories about Jesus were real. Luke was a physician and used his skills of science and reasoning to investigate and record his findings. Luke probably never previously knew, nor had heard, of Jesus. Luke did find Paul, who had an experience with the post-crucifixion Jesus. Luke gathered up information and stories from Paul and the Disciples and wrote what we now know as the Book of Luke. Luke also wrote the Book of Acts (of the Apostles).

So, the *disciples* were the *students* of Jesus. Then what are *apostles*? The word *apostle* comes from an ancient Greek word meaning *one is sent away*, or in other words is an *emissary* or *messenger*. Matthew, Mark, Luke, John and Paul are considered to be apostles, or messengers and emissaries of Jesus.

Theologians conflict over who wrote which Gospel first and if some of the Apostles used others' works to write their own works and letters. That discussion is topic for theology classes and entire textbooks. We do know the four Gospels do not correspond exactly with one another. This would be a normal circumstance. Try getting ten witnesses to explain something they saw and there will be ten variations of the same event.

Chapter 18
Harmony of the Gospels

Bible experts have examined each Gospel and broken them up
into discrete events. Then, these events have been compared
to the other three Gospels to yield a time line of the life of
Jesus. This comparison is called generically a "Harmony of
the Gospels". I am not going to include a complete one here,
but I will include an example in the table below:

Event or Location	*Matthew*	*Mark*	*Luke*	*John*
Feeding the 5000	14:15-21	6:35-44	9:12-17	6:4-13
Identification of Jesus as the Son of God				1:29-34
Banquet at Matthew's house	9:10-13	2:15-17	5:29-32	
Parable of the hidden treasure	13:44			

As you can see in the table above, these four examples are all
different as to which Apostles recorded them in their writings.
A student of the Bible can look at the whole Harmony and try
to establish a pattern as to what events each writer thought
was important. One thing which jumps out to me is that the
Apostle John tended to record the events which established

Edward F. LeGault

the **divinity** of Jesus, i.e., *Jesus is God, and our Lord.*
Sometimes the Gospels share the same materials, and some
times they don't. Some theologians beleve that some of the
writers of the Gospels used the other writers' materials, and
others don't. I personally believe since the Bible is written by
men, but is inspired by God, that there will be differences due
to the different experiences each disciple had with Jesus.

Chapter 19
Leadership

The original title of this chapter was going to be "Biblical Leadership" or "Christian Leadership." But, the leadership requirements made by our early leaders in the Christian church pretty much apply to any organization. There is a lot of controversy here and I will not get into the Christian legalities of marriage or divorce, or the specifics of rearing children. I will give some of my thoughts on why I think these were relevant then, and why they are still relevant now.

The first Bible quote (Eph 5:22-24) below is one of the **most** divisive verses for married couples. One has to step back and look at the entire Christian context to fully understand it. Even though many marriages attempt to be run with co-equal partners… in the eyes of the Lord, one party has to be responsible to God for all which happens in the home. The basis for Christian hierarchy is that Jesus Christ is the head of the Church. The husband of a marriage, which is blessed by God, has chosen to be responsible for his family before God. Jesus will sit at the right hand of God when we stand before Him for judgment. Husbands will stand before Jesus and be responsible for the unity of his home. Not the wife. The husband. This doesn't mean the husband cannot share responsibilities in the home. Everyone has different strengths and weaknesses. A marriage is a union of many strengths and many weaknesses. Two halves make a whole. Equal partners, but different responsibilities and duties.

"Wives, be subject to your own husbands, as to the Lord. For the husband is the head of the wife, and Christ also is the head of the assembly, being himself the savior of the body. But, as the assembly is subject to Christ, so let the wives also be to their own husbands in everything."
Eph 5:22-24

The next section is even more interesting:

"Husbands, love your wives, even as Christ also loved the assembly, and gave himself up for it... Even so, husbands also ought to love their own wives as their own bodies. He who loves his own wife loves himself. For no man ever hated his own flesh; but nourishes and cherishes it, even as the Lord also does the assembly... For this cause a man will leave his father and mother, and will be joined to his wife. The two will become one flesh... Nevertheless each of you must also love his own wife even as himself; and let the wife see that she respects her husband."
Ephesians 25-33

This has been a puzzling passage for many people. Why wouldn't a husband love his wife? Or, why would a man love their body so much more than their wife?

This is one of those cases where a student must look back in time at the ancient culture and society, rather than our culture and society today. Back then, 2000 years ago, men and women were often joined in marriage by family or political agreements.

This was the old method of the matchmaker and/or families joining together a man and a woman (via their children) for financial or political reasons. And sometimes, men took wives because the woman was a widow and her dead husband's brother, or other male relative, was obligated to take the widow as a wife. (See the book of Ruth in the Old Testament). This allowed the wife to bear children in the husband's lineage and name. It also kept their money, land, businesses, livestock, etc., in the former husband's family. They were a clan-centered society back then. Today, we are more individual centered… I almost said self-centered, but that seems a bit strong. Marriage did not always happen for "love". That is a fairly recent evolution in Western civilization.

But, what about outside the marriage and home? What ancient requirements did our Jewish and Christian ancestors believe were necessary to be leaders?

"This is a faithful saying: if a man seeks the office of an overseer, he desires a good work. The overseer therefore must be without reproach, the husband of one wife, temperate, sensible, modest, hospitable, good at teaching; not a drinker, not violent, not greedy for money, but gentle, not quarrelsome, not covetous; one who rules his own house well, having children in subjection with all reverence; but if a man doesn't know how to rule his own house, how will he take care of the assembly of God? Not a new convert, lest being puffed up he fall into the same condemnation as the devil. Moreover he must have good testimony from those who are

outside, to avoid falling into reproach and the snare of the devil. Servants, in the same way, must be reverent, not double-tongued, not addicted to much wine, not greedy for money; holding the mystery of the faith in a pure conscience. Let them also first be tested; then let them serve if they are blameless. Their wives in the same way must be reverent, not slanderers, temperate, faithful in all things. Let servants be husbands of one wife, ruling their children and their own houses well."
1 Tim 3:1-12

"I left you in Crete for this reason, that you would set in order the things that were lacking, and appoint elders in every city, as I directed you; if anyone is blameless, the husband of one wife, having children who believe, who are not accused of loose or unruly behavior. For the overseer must be blameless, as God's steward; not self-pleasing, not easily angered, not given to wine, not violent, not greedy for dishonest gain; but, given to hospitality, a lover of good, sober minded, fair, holy, self-controlled; holding to the faithful word which is according to the teaching, that he may be able to exhort in the sound doctrine, and to convict those who contradict him."
Titus 1:5-9

I went through these two passages and pulled out the generic characteristics, or qualities, of leaders (masters) and followers (slaves), and also qualities for wives. I am going to leave out the "religious" requirements and just list the generic qualities:

- without reproach
- sensible
- modest
- hospitable
- good at teaching
- not violent

- not greedy
- gentle
- not quarrelsome
- not covetous
- not puffed up
- receives good testimony from others
- reverent
- not double-tongued
- not addicted to much wine
- not slanderous
- temperate
- not easily angered
- a lover of good
- sober minded
- fair
- self-controlled

These are the qualities I want for our politicians and government leaders, for my employer, for my workers, for my wife and children, for the man who will marry my daughter, and the people who are my neighbors. Not all of them are leader qualities in the traditional sense, but these are good characteristics of the people I want to be around me… How about you?

And, if you are looking for a spouse, then these are the same qualities you should be looking for… not necessarily specific physical attributes (is he tall enough?, is she beautiful?, etc.). With age, physical attributes harden, sag and blur… but, characteristics and qualities of your personality and soul linger on into your afterlife.

Edward F. LeGault

Chapter 20
Fatherhood

[Author's Note: This chapter is adapted from one of my Fathers' Day Sermons.]

I am going to write a few words about how to be the father which God wants me to be.

I remember getting married. The time we spent in pre-marriage classes at the church. The counseling with our pastor. All the planning. Well, my wife-to-be did most of the planning:

- The bridal shows which I did NOT want to attend.
- The cake testing.
- Her dress shopping.
- It was actually kind of like she had another full-time job.

My main job was mainly to just show up and say a few pre-selected words at the wedding ceremony. Pretty easy.
A few years later our daughter, Kathleen, was born. My wife

Edward F. LeGault

and I had taken the usual hospital birthing classes.

She learning how to breathe.... and my coaching her to breathe and push. When the time for the baby's delivery had arrived, my wife did all the work... and my job was to show up at the hospital and say a few encouraging words. Pretty easy.

I remember holding my tiny newborn daughter there in the hospital delivery room and thinking, "WOW! This is really a great miracle and gift from God!" ...and then reality and fear set in. **"What. Do. I. Do. Now?!"**

Let me digress a little. Usually when I need to learn something new for work, or at home, I read some books or magazines on the appropriate subject specialty area.

I collect a lot of books. On just about any subject from cooking to carpentry to computers to car repair to gardening. And a lot more.

When I needed to know how to raise a child? Easy... read some books!

So I bought some more books. On feeding. Changing diapers. On child discipline. How to be the perfect parent. And many more subjects. It seems as if there is an unending supply of reading material on the subject of children rearing.

Sometimes, though, I forget to check into the ultimate parenting guide: ***The Bible***

Let's see what God has to say about fatherhood.
In the beginning, as recorded in the book of Genesis, were the

first couple -- Adam and Eve. I think we all know the story of Adam and Eve and the forbidden fruit in the Garden of Eden. Adam let Eve talk him into doing something pretty stupid that he *knew* was wrong. (But, after all, Eve was the best looking woman on the planet! And how could he resist!).

Adam didn't obey God and consequently they (Adam & Eve) ended up getting evicted from their perfect home. Adam knew what he was doing was wrong when he disobeyed God's directions. Yet, he evidently needed to follow the misdirection of the most beautiful woman he had ever known.

Fathers, let me remind you to *follow your conscience,* even when influenced by other members of your family. That little voice in your head telling you what you are doing is wrong just might be God giving you hints for a better and smarter life.

The **first lesson** we learn, as Dads, is *we need to obey God* in **all** of his instructions (it's not multiple choice!)

Let's think about the immediate consequences in which our first two humans found themselves. Adam and his wife, Eve, suddenly *had no shelter or food.* They were technically, after all, homeless. Literally, all they had were the clothes they were wearing... and those had been provided by God.

Reading from Genesis chapter 3, verses 17-19 we learn,

To Adam God said, "Because you listened to your wife and ate from the tree about which I commanded **you,** *'You must not eat of it,' therefore "Cursed is the ground because of you; through* **painful toil** *you will eat of it all the days of your life. It will produce* **thorns and thistles** *for you and you will eat*

Edward F. LeGault

*the plants of the field. By the **sweat of your brow** you will eat your food until you return to the ground, since from it you were taken; for dust you are and to dust you will return."*
[Note: emphasis added]

Think about it. Adam and Eve had lived the good, easy life in the Garden of Eden. Now, they were suddenly on their own in a whole new frontier: thistles, thorns, weeds and all. Adam had no special skills. But, he now had to do everything. Build a shelter, find and raise food, repair and replace their clothing. That was going to be a lot of hard work!

Their life in the Garden of Eden probably did not prepare them for the rigors of the world outside. But, they had to do more than just survive. There would be a family (indeed a whole new people) to raise... rules, laws and traditions to establish... At the same time Adam had to discover or figure out how to feed, cloth and provide shelter for his family, and those to follow. I don't think Adam realized how hard the work was going to be as he left the Garden.

Lesson #2: Dads, we need to work hard to provide for and *stay true to our family.*

Let's look at another father in the Bible. In Genesis chapter 15, verse 5, God made a covenant (or promise) with Abraham:

God took Abraham outside and said, "Look up at the heavens and count the stars – if indeed you can count them." Then God said to Abraham, "So shall your offspring be."

God was telling Abraham he would have many descendants. But, to Abraham and his wife Sarah there was a major problem. We must remember Abraham and Sarah were **really** old.... Sarah was well past the normal age of child-bearing and hadn't yet had any children. Sarah was considered to be barren, i.e., unable to have any children. So Sarah took things in her own hands to provide a son for Abraham. She arranged a sexual affair for Abraham with another woman.

But that was not what God had in mind (and consequently that has caused all kinds of problems in the Middle East, and now the world). Fathers -- remember my point number one, to follow your conscience? I am sure Abraham *knew* in his heart and brain what he did with Sarah's servant, Hagar, was wrong. He forgot God had made a promise to him and Sarah.

Lesson #3: Dads, please *remember that promises are important...* not only does God keep His promises to us, but in our homes, our kids and wives **never,** never, ever forget those promises which we make to them!

Abraham and Sarah had to learn to be patient and obey the Lord to see the results of God's promise. Eventually their son Isaac was born.

Later, in chapter 22 of Genesis, God told Abraham to take his son, Isaac, along with some wood and fire, up on the mountainside to prepare a sacrifice. We know God was testing Abraham – big time! But, on the way up the mountain Isaac looks around and asks his dad, Abraham,

"Father? ... The fire and wood are here," ... "but where is the lamb for the burnt offering?"
Genesis 22:7

You know what? --- Isaac was very observant. Kids are like that. They see and notice things about the way we lead our own lives. They remember the broken promises. They also remember the good and the bad times in their childhood. Just remember… *they remember.*

Lesson # 4: Dads, be aware that our *kids notice all the little things that we do...*

Back to our story of Abraham and Isaac.

Abraham answered, "God himself will provide the lamb for the burnt offering, my son." And the two of them went on together.
Genesis 22:8

This is a standard Sunday School class lesson on Abraham's obedience to God. Just as important, though, was the **attitude** of *Isaac*. As the two of them laid out the wood for fire together, Isaac did **not** run away. He wasn't stupid. He was putting 1+1 together, and the answer wasn't looking good. Then Abraham tied up Isaac onto the sacrificial alter. Isaac cooperated very willingly with his father.

After all, it was Isaac who was on the hot seat, so to speak. I know how I would have reacted – Abraham would have had to bind and gag me to get me on that alter!

But, Isaac must have noticed in his own daily life how his father, Abraham, had carefully followed God's lessons.

We know from scripture," *God provided a ram for the sacrifice, and Isaac was spared because of God's promise to Abraham."* Genesis 22:13-14

I believe Abraham had done a good job of raising-up Isaac as a Godly child. Isaac displayed a huge amount of faith and trust in the Lord. Otherwise, Isaac would have balked at being put on that sacrificial alter.

Lesson # 5: Dads, *raise-up your children right so they are equipped for the challenges of the world.*

We can't guarantee what our children will do when challenged by the forces of the world, but we can prepare them by reading and studying God's Word with them. God has given us his instruction book (the Bible) to prepare us for any situation we might encounter.

Let's now move on to lessons in the New Testament.

In chapter one of the Gospel of Matthew, Joseph of Nazareth learns about the pregnancy of Mary, his betrothed (or fiance). His choices, through this shame of her pregnancy out of legal wedlock, were to either have her stoned to death or to divorce her quietly. But an angel of the Lord appeared to Joseph in a dream. The angel told him what really had happened – Mary was carrying the Messiah child in her womb. Joseph decided to go ahead with the marriage and to raise this child. Joseph even seemed to treat Jesus as his own oldest son.

Jesus was known as a carpenter. Indeed, he was known as the *son* of a carpenter, just like his stepdad, Joseph. We can only assume Joseph trained Jesus as an apprentice in carpentry as any father would pass down his skills to his oldest son.

Lesson #6: *Fatherhood is more than a biological link.*

Adoptions. Blended families. Step children and even half-children. Can we really have half children? Didn't King

Edward F. LeGault

Solomon propose that? And the real mother in that story saw the impossible nature of that?

Fatherhood is a job description, *not a place on a genealogical chart.* I can attest to this. I was raised by a step-father who treated me as his oldest son --- all of the privileges and all of the extra responsibilities (like getting up at 5:00 am to feed the cows, horses, rabbits, stoke the wood fire, put on the pot of coffee, etc.)

In the Gospel of John, chapter 4, is recorded the miracle of Jesus healing the official's son.

*"Once more Jesus visited Cana in Galilee, where he had turned the water into wine. And there was a certain **royal official** whose son lay sick at Capernaum. When this man heard that Jesus had arrived in Galilee from Judea, he went to him and **begged** him to come and heal his son, who was close to death."*
John 4: 46-47

This is an interesting passage. Historically we know that in the city of Capernaum there was a Roman customs station and, indeed, the residence of a high officer of the king. There was also a detachment of Roman soldiers stationed there. This royal official, or nobleman, who was referenced, was most likely a member of the court of Herod Antipas. (His name was probably not mentioned to protect him and his family). *The inhabitants of Capernaum were known for their excessive pride.*

The disease mentioned here was one of a high fever -- probably something like malaria or typhoid. The Greek words here, the verb *mello*, with *teleutau*, indeed meant that this official's son was *right at the verge of death.* Remember this nobleman had access to the best Roman health care available in Capernaum... all to no avail.

Somehow this nobleman had heard of the Jewish miracle healer. He could very well have sent a messenger to ask Jesus to come to the palace... or he could even have sent a squad of Roman soldiers to forcefully bring Jesus back to him. Instead, the nobleman went himself, *in humility,* and *begged* Jesus to come back with him and heal his son.

Jesus looked inside this man's heart and told him to go home... his son was healed.
(From John 4:50)

So men, **lesson #7** is: *being humble has many rewards.*

[By the way, some Bible commentaries think this nobleman's wife was converted to a believer in Christ on this occasion and afterward became a dedicated follower of Jesus. She may have been the wife of Cuza mentioned in Luke 8:3 as one of the women attending to Jesus.]

One of the greatest rewards men can have is working in a childrens ministry. Being humble. Getting down on the floor teaching and playing with the preschoolers. Or, jumping and singing loudly with the elementary kids. Don't worry about making a fool of yourself around the children... just have fun and help do God's work.

Or sometimes being humble means swallowing your pride and telling your children you were wrong or that you made a mistake.
My daughter jokingly refers to her Dad as "perfect." Well

Edward F. LeGault

Kathleen, I do make mistakes. I remember the time my hands looked like an art project gone wrong. I had attempted a quick job of replacing the four color ink cartridges in our computer printer at home – black, blue, red, and yellow ink. Now, I am always telling Kathleen to think first, then to think again, and then finally do whatever she is attempting. **I** made the mistake of not thinking and **I** put the blue ink cartridge in the yellow ink slot... *just for a few seconds,* but enough time for the old ink to mix with some of the new ink... blue plus yellow equals green! I spent an hour cleaning up the mess trying to get yellow to print instead of green...

Fathers, let us remember that Christian character in our children comes from the Holy Spirit, NOT by mere parental discipline. We must model virtue and act in obedience to the Lord. In Galatians 6:22, the apostle Paul wrote about the fruit of the Spirit. I pray my walk with the Lord will be apparent to my family, will teach my family, and with **my** practice will become apparent that I have learned these Christian virtues of the fruit of the Spirit and passed them on to my daughter and the other children in the Church whose lives I touch.

The fruit of the Spirit or virtues are:

joy,
love,
peace,
patience,
kindness,
goodness,
gentleness,
faithfulness,
and self-control.

Dads, we can't do it alone. It takes more than our actions to raise-up our children in a Godly manner. We must turn to prayer for help from the Holy Spirit.

Lesson # 8: Dads, *we can't do it alone; Prayer helps a great deal.*

Fathers, what does this mean to us today?

Here are a few words for the women out there: (men close your ears and eyes for a few moments) Ladies, we need your help! We men can't do it alone. Of course, you women already know that... I just thought I would remind the men here. *That is why God made women... to get things done!* They help us to keep focused on what is right. Help us raise our children in the manner God wants us to, etc.

Now parents, I haven't brought to you some secret formula for raising-up Godly children. *Sometimes, no matter how hard we try or how much praying we do, sometimes a child will disappoint us.*

We have some friends, Bob and Joan (names changed to protect the innocent). They raised their children in a good loving home – complete with church activities and youth ministries. However, they have a daughter who as a teenager decided to rebel. They came to the end of their ropes and had her admitted to one of those "tough love" residential wilderness camps for therapy and counseling. The long term verdict I believe was successful.

We have another friend with a daughter about the same age as ours. Her mother and father both have a history of alcohol and drug abuse. She was a rebelling teenager. She spent part of her summer vacations in residential wilderness camps for counseling and therapy. She is now a successful college student, working, and dreaming about her own business someday.

We have some friends – in fact he is a minister – who raised their children in all the right "Christian" ways. However, this couple had a rebellious teenage daughter who left home to live with her boyfriend. The minister felt he was a failure as a Christian parent and leader and so he submitted his resignation to his church Board of Elders…

Looking at God's book (the Bible), how do we deal with rebellious children?

Starting at Luke 15:11, Jesus illustrates this point with the story of the "Prodigal Son."

"A man had two sons. When the younger told his father, 'I want my share of your estate now, instead of waiting until you die!' His father agreed to divide his wealth between his sons.

A few days later this younger son packed all his belongings and took a trip to a distant land, and there he wasted all his money on parties and prostitutes. About the time his money was gone a great famine swept over the land, and he began to starve. He persuaded a local farmer to hire him to feed his pigs. The boy became so hungry that even the pods he was feeding the swine looked good to him. And no one gave him anything to eat.

When he finally came to his senses, he said to himself, 'At home even the hired men have food enough and to spare, and here I am, dying of hunger! I will go home to my father and say, "Father, I have sinned against both heaven and you, and am no longer worthy of being called your son. Please take me on as a hired man."'

So he returned home to his father. **And while he was still a long distance away, his father saw him coming,** *and* (his father) *was filled with loving pity and ran and embraced him and kissed him.*

His son said to him, 'Father, I have sinned against heaven and you, and am not worthy of being called your son.'

But his father said to the slaves, 'Quick! Bring the finest robe in the house and put it on him. And a jeweled ring for his finger; and shoes! And kill the calf we have in the fattening pen. We must celebrate with a feast, for this son of mine was dead and has returned to life. He was lost and is found'". (So the celebration began...)
Luke 15:11-32

Notice that the father had been watching for and hoping his son would return some day.

Let's now return to the story of the minister's family and their wayward daughter.

The Board of Elders at that church refused to accept the resignation of the pastor; for they knew that he and his wife had done everything they could to raise their daughter properly in a Christian home. The board told him to go home and continue to be the father who God wanted him to be.

The girl's parents discussed the issue and decided they had

made the right decision of not approving of their wayward daughter's lifestyle. However, they decided to keep the lines of communication open with their daughter. She could call home any time to talk to her parents. Also, she was invited to dinner (but not her live-in boyfriend) at the weekly family dinners. Some weeks she came for dinner and some weeks she didn't come around. Her parents continued to show their love for their daughter. But, the daughter knew her parents disapproved of her lifestyle choices.

Out of the blue one week, the parents received the phone call which they had prayed for, but never really expected to get. Their daughter wanted to come home! She had realized the wrongs she had committed against God and her parents, and wanted to start over. The prodigal daughter had rejected the ways of the world!

Lesson # 9: Men (and ladies, too), *parenthood ain't easy – it's down right hard work.* It's emotionally difficult. At times, Christian parenthood is radically different from what the rest of the world is doing. It is also expensive in more ways than one.

The world has other preoccupations with parenthood. I am going to lighten this up a little before wrapping things up.

I heard a news report some time ago that it is very expensive to raise a child in our society today. No kidding! That particular year's figure was that it takes in excess of over $160,000 to raise one child. The good news is you probably get a slight discount for multiple children because of the savings through hand-me-down clothes, toys and stuff.

If we didn't have kids, what could $160,000 buy?

- In most of the country you could buy a modest 3 bedroom, 2 bath home on a large lot in the suburbs;
- Or, two or three very nice cars;
- Or, a pretty good used light airplane;
- Or a really nice boat;
- Or a nice really RV for traveling around the country.

I think you get the picture.

...So dads, what do we get for our $160,000 investment? I don't know about you, but here is what I get from it and what it is worth to me:

1) Like I told you earlier, I remember that day in August, a long time ago, at about 8:30 in the morning when the doctor at O'Connor Hospital, in San Jose, held up for **my** view **my** new baby daughter -- how small and awesome and beautiful she looked (value of that = Priceless).

2) I remember her learning to roll, crawl, walk and talk (value of that = Priceless).

3) I remember taking our daughter to Disneyland for her first time on her third birthday. She was awestruck by the performance of the mechanical birds in the *Tiki Room*. Next we took the *Pirates of the Caribbean* ride. At that first big plunge down into the darkness she started screaming and crying -- she wanted out of that boat right NOW! She did NOT like that ride. We had our hands full calming her down until the end of the ride and just trying to keep her in the boat. Then as we were preparing to get out of the boat at the end of the ride, Kathleen turned to me and said, "Daddy, lets do that again!" (value of that = Priceless).

Edward F. LeGault

4) I remember many a night when Kathleen was sick and I
held her on my lap in a rocking chair or recliner in a pile of
blankets and pillows trying to get her comfortable so she
could fall asleep (value of that = Priceless).

5) Whenever she had a cut or splinter she came to "Doctor
Daddy" for First Aid (value of that = Priceless).

6) I looked forward to her bringing that first boyfriend home
on that first date, and my taking him aside to get to know
something about him. I did inform him of my background
– Vietnam Veteran, Expert Rifle Marksman, NRA certified
instructor on all manner of firearms. Then I told him that if
he should break my princess's heart that she would
probably get over it, but I wouldn't. The look on his face –
it was Priceless!

7) Earning her Girl Scout Gold Award. There were many
years when her mother and I were Girl Scout leaders (yes,
even me). Lots of work. In Junior High she worked on a
small project and earned her Silver Award. Then in High
School, she worked on a major public service project at a
local elementary school. Lots of planning on her part. Lots
of hard work. I was very proud and honored when she was
presented with her Girl Scout Gold Award. That entire
experience was, indeed, Priceless!

8) She graduated from our local community college through a
lot of work with art and transfer degrees. That was
Priceless. As I was writing the first edition of this book, we
were planning our college campus visitation trip one
summer. The look in her eyes and her enthusiasm as she
chose which university to apply to was priceless – she has
grown up and becoming her own woman. [Note: as I am
writing this update she is in her last quarter at Central
Washington University preparing to graduate with a

Bachelors of Fine Arts degree in Studio Arts… she is now a professional artist. Watching her cross the stage in her cap and gown will be Priceless!]

9) Hopefully, one day I'll walk her down the aisle at her wedding – that will indeed be Priceless.

…And some day after some separation of time we'll meet in Heaven for all eternity with God – that will truly be priceless...

Lesson # 10: To paraphrase a well-known credit card ad – Some things cost money ($160,000/child) but, *the really great events in the life of a Dad (and Mom) are way beyond measurement – they are indeed priceless.*

There is one more Dad I would like to tell you about. He is the most loving, caring and forgiving Father around.

This particular Father gave his children everything. The best home, the best food. They didn't even have to work hard for a living. This Father I am referring to visited with his grown children on a regular basis. He was pretty easy going and loved His children very much.

But His children turned their backs on Him and followed the wrong crowd. The kids listened to the lies and deceit of someone trying to be a home-wrecker. They forgot the love their Father had for them. They forgot that their Father had given them everything, even their very lives.

They disobeyed their Father and ended up deep in debt and paying the consequences -- They were even banished to another land where they were separated from their Father. The estranged children had their own children and the grandkids weren't any better than their parents. Nor were the great grandkids, or the generations after that.

What did their Father do? First of all, his love **never** ended. He had even forgiven what they had done. The problem was He wanted them to see their own short-comings and come back to Him willingly. The Father monitored their progress, or lack of it, over the years. He let them wander aimlessly in life for a long time (sometimes in the desert or wilderness). He was waiting and watching them get deeper and deeper into trouble. Finally one day this Father decided that **enough was enough** – He missed His children and wanted to be re-united with them. He sent a Son to pay for their debts and misdeeds. This was unusual because the other children weren't just misguided or misdirected... some of them had done some really bad nasty stuff. This Father's other children and their descendants had actually earned the death penalty for all of the bad things they had done. But, the Father had one true Son who volunteered to pay the price for all of the rest of the family. That one Son died a terrible death to free the rest of His family from bondage.

You see, I am talking about God, the Father, and His Son. Jesus Christ paid the ultimate price with His life so we can have everlasting Life with God, our Father.

Lesson #11:
"For God so loved the world, that He gave His only begotten Son, that whoever believes in Him should not perish, but should be saved through Him."
John 3:16

Let's pray.

Lord, I thank for the privilege of being both someone's child and someone's parent. I pray for all of the parent-child relationships reading or listening to these words. I know there are good relationships here and I thank you and praise you for them.

I also know there are some here who are hurting in their relationships with either their children or their parents. I pray for healing for those hurting relationships. And thank you, Father, for the relationship you make possible for us through your Son, Jesus Christ.

And now, if there are some here who are reading or listening to these words who have not yet taken the opportunity to be part of God's family and accept Jesus Christ into your heart, then perhaps now you can say this prayer silently in your heart with me:

Dear Heavenly Father. You are the only true Father. Thank you for your patience in tending to us, Your flock, Your children. You knew us even before we were born. You know what is truly in our hearts. You know all of our hurts and pains. You know what we think and do, yet still You love us... Even though we don't deserve your love.

I know there is a sacrificial penalty to pay for our sins against You. Yet, we can never fulfill that sacrificial role. Thank you for sending your own Son, Jesus Christ, to pay the penalty for all that we sin against You. There are some here reading and listening to these words who have known You for some time. And I thank You for that love which You have shown them. Lord Jesus, there may be some here reading and listening to these words who have doubts about You, maybe they have even rejected You in the past. By the Grace of God, I pray for

Edward F. LeGault

the Holy Spirit to enter into their hearts and to lead them in a life seeking Your love, Your truth, and Your forgiveness. I pray they will place their faith in Jesus Christ as their Lord and Savior.

Thank you, in the name of the Father, the Son, and Holy Spirit.

Amen.

Chapter 21
State of the Christian Church

The collapse of the Soviet Union style of Communism and the
end of the Cold War in the late twentieth century created a
power vacuum among the ethnic, religious, regional and
national leaders in a large part of the world. A population
explosion is radically changing the population centers of parts
of Europe and Asia. Islam is a fast growing culture spreading
throughout the world. And the violence of the radical Muslim
Jihadists are threatening the very foundation of Western
civilization through the rapid spread of Islam and their
demands for non-Muslims to bow down to Islam and Shariah
Law.

Many large Christian denominations are shrinking. The
number of Western missionaries is decreasing while their age
is increasing. There is a shortage of Roman Catholic priests.
Ministries are switching from the clergy to lay leaders (very
Biblical, though). Churches are merging or closing. Many are
even going bankrupt. Global democratization has lessened the
power and influence of the traditional Christian churches and
other Christian institutions. The geographic center of

Edward F. LeGault

Christianity is moving from north and west (USA and Western Europe) to south and east (South America and Asia/Africa). The new Christian Church fits its local customs more while it is has fewer traditional ceremonies and customs of the old Church.

Older Christian denominations are losing membership and attendance. There has been a switch from the small neighborhood, or rural church, to the huge mega-churches. These larger mega-churches are replacing the functions of denominations, schools, Bible colleges, training centers, radio/television stations and even publishing houses.

The Protestant Ethic and Christian Bible literacy is quickly disappearing. Public schools in the U.S. can no longer teach or hold the concept of absolute rights and wrongs. Everything is "relative" to the individual person experiencing their own life. The different generations think, work, and act differently.

The "greatest" generation – those who fought and lived through World War II had made great sacrifices for their country. They then rebuilt America and the world after the war. That generation went from seeing (or hearing) Lindbergh's solo crossing of the Atlantic Ocean to experiencing common daily flights on jet-powered mega-size airliners cruising through the skies around the world. Even witnessed flights into outer space and to the moon.

Today's young men and women (and my daughter is one of them) grew up with many things which did not even exist when their grandparents and great-grandparents were their age: cell phones (not even dial telephones), television, air travel, mp3 music players, computers (especially not handheld tablets), video games, the Internet, social media, etc. Whole classes of things have come and gone: rotary telephones (try to find a pay phone booth!), adding machines (not calculators), telephone answering machines, fax machines, typewriters (both manual and electric), Polaroid cameras, the little flash cubes atop 126 film cameras, reel to reel tape, 8 track, and cassette recorders… and many more.

I think back and remember that my daughter has always had a personal computer in the home (either mine or hers) and the ability to play movies and cartoons on demand at home on a television (VHS tape, DVD, movies on demand, etc).

All of these "distractions" means less family time and less interaction with others *unless* a concerted effort is made to get out of the house and to socialize with others in the local community. This carries over to the Church. Less time for church activities. Less time for Bible study and learning. Too many other distractions.

So, what we end up with is many different generations of people who have different experiences, education, skills, needs, expectations, etc., trying to find the meaning to life at the same time at the same places. Different needs for different peoples. Each person in each of these groups thinks and learns differently, at different paces. The challenge in the churches today is how to serve all of these different peoples with different needs and still spread the message of the Gospel to the rest of the peoples of the world.

Edward F. LeGault

Chapter 22
Prayer

Prayer is our method of communicating with God. Unfortunately, many of us tend to ask things of God, and then we are not in tune to receive His answer. God **always** answers our prayers. The answer might not be what we want to hear. We might not be listening or paying attention and miss His answer altogether.

So, how then do we pray? It is not hard. Let's look at a couple of examples from the Bible.

<u>A Psalm by David</u>

"The Lord is my shepherd: I shall lack nothing.
He makes me lie down in green pastures.
He leads me beside still waters.
He restores my soul.
He guides me in the paths of righteousness for His name's sake.
Even though I walk through the valley of the shadow of death,
I will fear no evil, for You are with me.

Edward F. LeGault

Your rod and your staff, they comfort me.
You prepare a table before me in the presence of my enemies.
You anoint my head with oil.
My cup runs over.
Surely goodness and loving kindness shall follow me all the
days of my life, and I will dwell in the Lord's house forever."
Psalm 23

The Lord's Prayer

When he (Jesus) finished praying in a certain place, one of his
disciples said to him, "Lord, teach us to pray, just as John (the
Baptizer) also taught his disciples."
He (Jesus) said to them:

"When you pray, say,
Our Father, which art in heaven,
hallowed be thy name;
thy kingdom come;
thy will be done,
On earth as it is in heaven.
Give us this day our daily bread.
And forgive us our trespasses,
As we forgive those that trespass against us.
And lead us not into temptation;
But deliver us from evil."

[Note: later added] *For thine is the kingdom,*
The power, and the glory,
For ever and ever.

Amen.

Note: This is from a combination of passages from Luke 11:1-2a and Matthew 6:9-13)

Using the Lord's Prayer instruction from Jesus we can simplify prayer instruction to this:

P – Praise the Lord.
R – Remember something God has done for you.
A – Ask God for what you think you want.
Y – Yield to God in His name

Further instruction from Jesus:

"Ask, and it will be given you. Seek, and you will find. Knock, and it will be opened for you. For everyone who asks, receives. He who seeks, finds. To him who knocks, it will be opened. Or who is there among you, who, if his son asks him for bread, will give him a stone? Or if he asks for a fish, who will give him a serpent? If you then, being evil, know how to give good gifts to your children, how much more will your Father, who is in heaven, give good things to those who ask him!"
- Matthew 7:7-11

Edward F. LeGault

Chapter 23
Why do bad things happen to good people?

I was proof reading my second edition of this manuscript and I thought I was pretty much done with it. My wife and I video-communicate ("Skype") with our daughter at least a couple of times a week. As I write this she is just finishing her last quarter of fine arts studies at Central Washington University.

A few days ago when we called her, she didn't look so well on the video screen. Usually she is full of joy as she is finishing her last couple of classes and getting ready for her Senior Art Gallery Show and her upcoming college group history class trip to Rome, Italy.

But, the first thing she said was the day had not been good at all. She told us about a graduate student in her department who had passed away the night before after being hospitalized for a week with pneumonia. A great cloud of sadness had settled over her art department.

In times like this a question arises, "Why do bad things

happen to good people?"

When I was in my early teens, a logger friend of my Dad, and his young daughter, were killed in a freak accident one cold winter day cutting firewood. He was felling a frozen tree and it split and snapped back into both of them. Outside of the previous loss of a few old family members, that was my first experience with losing someone I personally knew. Sadly, it has been so long ago I can't even remember the girl's name, though at the time we were fairly good friends. I was at a loss as to why something so bad could happen to someone so young and innocent. All I can say is Rest in Peace (RIP).

We lost a friend in my high school graduation class. Dave was killed in a sledding accident, if I remember correctly. It was not only sad, it struck us that we were not immortal. Young people always believe they are "bullet proof". The war in Vietnam was still going and we lost a few more there, after graduation, in the service of their country. While not all right... a loss is a loss, but to lose one before he even graduated from high school seemed so sudden and strange. RIP Dave.

One of the greatest losses a person can suffer is losing a child. It is devastating to a parent to have to bury one of their children. A few years ago we lost a nephew in a vehicle accident. Brian was young and left behind a grieving widow. Why?, Lord, why? Being the "churched" one in the family I couldn't give a reason to his father, my brother, why such a tragedy should occur. Sure, there was probably someone else or something else to blame. But still, that does not make it better for his surviving family and friends. Why would our loving God let someone so young be killed in an accident where someone else was at fault? RIP Brian.

This book is dedicated to John Dawson, who I considered to be my best guy friend. He, like all of us, had his problems. But, in the end, he was a Godly man. John was always there when we needed his help. He died a terrible, painful death by some sort of stomach cancer. He was too young to die, and he left behind a widow and two sons. RIP John.

Why would God let bad things happen to good people? I have to turn to the Bible for clues to that question.

In the Old Testament, Moses was given the task of freeing God's people, the Israelites, from slavery under the Egyptian Pharaoh. Moses was faithful and dependent upon the Lord for the Israelites' survival. Even when the peoples of the Israelite tribes turned away from God, Moses stayed true to the Lord, God... Except one time when the Israelites needed water and Moses did not follow God's instructions... Moses struck a rock wall with his staff and water poured forth.

Moses had disobeyed God (Moses was supposed to speak to the rock). Because of that one little act of non-obedience, God told Moses that he (Moses) would not lead his people into the promised land. Moses had to watch from a mountain as Joshua, his helper, led the Israelites across the Jordan River into the Promised Land.

The consequences of that one act of disobedience to God, I would imagine, just about broke Moses' heart. I am not saying that disobeying God, or sinning, is the cause of bad things happening to us. Though some people believe this idea, Christ's death on the cross paid for our sins, and there is no basis for believing God makes bad things happen to those who sin.

Edward F. LeGault

Let's look at the story of Job from the Old Testament. Job was a successful, rich man with a good family, who was faithfull to God:

"There was a man in the land of Uz, whose name was Job. That man was blameless and upright, and one who feared God, and turned away from evil. There were born to him seven sons and three daughters. His possessions also were seven thousand sheep, three thousand camels, five hundred yoke of oxen, five hundred female donkeys, and a very great household..."

He was a favorite servant of God who made a "bet" with the devil:

"...Yahweh said to Satan, 'Have you considered my servant, Job? For there is no one like him in the earth, a blameless and an upright man, one who fears God, and turns away from evil.'" Then Satan answered Yahweh, and said, *'Does Job fear God for nothing? Haven't you made a hedge around him, and around his house, and around all that he has, on every side? You have blessed the work of his hands, and his substance is increased in the land. But stretch out your hand now, and touch all that he has, and he will renounce you to your face.'"*

God (Yahweh) knew Job was a man strong in his faith:

"Yahweh said to Satan, 'Behold, all that he has is in your power. Only on himself don't stretch out your hand.'"

So God (Yahweh) let Satan have his way with Job:

"...There came a messenger to Job, and said, 'The oxen were plowing, and the donkeys feeding beside them, and the Sabeans

attacked, and took them away. Yes, they have killed the servants
with the edge of the sword, and I alone have escaped to tell you.'
While he was still speaking, there also came another, and said, 'The
fire of God has fallen from the sky, and has burned up the sheep
and the servants, and consumed them, and I alone have escaped to
tell you.' While he was still speaking, there came also another, and
said, 'The Chaldeans made three bands, and swept down on the
camels, and have taken them away, yes, and killed the servants
with the edge of the sword; and I alone have escaped to tell you.'
While he was still speaking, there came also another, and said,
'Your sons and your daughters were eating and drinking wine in
their oldest brother's house, and behold, there came a great wind
from the wilderness, and struck the four corners of the house, and it
fell on the young men, and they are dead. I alone have escaped to
tell you...' "

In just a matter of days, nearly everything Job held dear was
gone or destroyed. He lost his wealth, his family and his
property. What more could happen? God let Satan mess with
Job's health, afflicting Job with a terrible skin disease…
probably leprosy. Through all these trials and tribulations, Job
never blamed God for his problems. There is a lot more to the
story, but in the end:

"Yahweh gave Job twice as much as he had before. Then
came there to him all his brothers, and all his sisters, and all
those who had been of his acquaintance before, and ate bread
with him in his house. They comforted him, and consoled him
concerning all the evil that Yahweh had brought on him.
Everyone also gave him a piece of money, and everyone a
ring of gold. So Yahweh blessed the latter end of Job more
than his beginning. He had fourteen thousand sheep, six
thousand camels, one thousand yoke of oxen, and a thousand
female donkeys. He had also seven sons and three (beautiful)

Edward F. LeGault

daughters."

Job stayed faithful to the Lord and the Lord restored all he had, and more.

In the New Testament, we have the recorded stories of the Apostle Paul. Let me just say that Paul had been a well-to-do Roman-born citizen known as Saul who had been terrifying the followers of Jesus after the Resurrection. One day, out on the road, Saul had a close encounter with the resurrected Jesus. He became a new man... transformed by his experience with Jesus who gave him a new name of Paul. Paul paid heavily for being a follower of Jesus. He was beaten, starved, shipwrecked, bitten by a poisonous snake, imprisoned and sentenced to death. He suffered from some unknown "thorn in his side". But, like Job he never wavered in his love for God.

I have known people who had the good life and then lost jobs, their family and even their health… and yet they shined with their faith and hope in the Lord. Some get through the bad times and grow and learn from their suffering, with their faith giving them strength. Others don't and sometimes even reject God… and remain bitter. Which life would you prefer: bitterness or hope?

So we come back the original question: Why do bad things happen to good people? I don't know. Nobody does. I believe all things happen for a reason which only God knows. I also believe that God will always answer our prayers, if only we turn our attention and focus to the Lord. Even in the darkest of times we must have faith in God.

Chapter 24
Doxology

A doxology is a short hymn sung as an expression of praise to the Holy Trinity (God): The Father, the Son and the Holy Spirit (Holy Ghost).

Here is a popular doxology often used to end a Christian church service, Bible study or a Christian theology class, and in this case, this book:

Praise God, from whom all blessings flow;
Praise him, all creatures here below;
Praise him above, ye heavenly host;
Praise Father, Son, and Holy Ghost.
Amen.

Edward F. LeGault

Appendix 1
Works Used for Research

Dummelow, J.R., editor. The One Volume Bible Commentary. Macmillan, 1936.

Evangelical Dictionary of Theology. Baker Books, 1984. From BibleSoft CD, 2002.

McClintock and Strong Encyclopedia. Electronic Database, 2000. BibleSoft CD 2002.

Nelson's Illustrated Bible Dictionary, Thomas Nelson Publishers, 1986, BibleSoft CD, 2002

New International Version Bible. Online edition: Bible Gateway, www.Gospelcom.net.

New Unger's Bible Dictionary. Moody Press, 1988. From BibleSoft CD, 2002.

Wycliffe Bible Commentary. Moody Press, 1962. From BibleSoft CD, 2002.

Vine's Expository Dictionary of Biblical Words. Thomas Nelson, 1985. From BibleSoft CD ver 3.3A, 2002.

World English Bible. Anonymous (various researchers), down loadable from The Gutenberg Project, www.Gutenberg.org

Edward F. LeGault

Appendix 2
Suggested books for further reading:

In the midst of World War II, England was under heavy aerial attack from the Nazi air forces. Hope was almost lost. BBC radio called upon C.S. Lewis, a professor of Medieval and Renaissance literature at Cambridge University, to conduct a series of radio programs to encourage Britons to have hope during their darkest hours. The text of those radio programs were printed as three small books, and eventually compiled into one complete book: *Mere Christianity*, by C.S. Lewis.

A more contemporary book was written by an investigative journalist. His results of his personal investigation into the evidence for Jesus Christ surprised that author. Read *The Case for Christ* by Lee Strobel.

Condensed into 31 chapters, a high level continuous story of the Bible, from Genesis to Revelation is easy reading. Not a Bible, but there is a Bible study available and the book itself has discussion questions at the back of the book for your study. The Story: The Bible as One Continuing Story of God and His People. Published by Zondervan. Foreword by Max Lucado and Randy Frazee.

Edward F. LeGault

Appendix 3
Recommended Bible translations:

The NET Bible: The NET Bible (New English Translation) is a completely new translation of the Bible with 60,932 translators' notes. It was completed by more than 25 scholars – experts in the original biblical languages – who worked directly from the best currently available Hebrew, Aramaic, and Greek texts. Available in print, down loadable and online versions, www.netbible.com

The WEB Bible (World English Bible): is a Public Domain (no copyright) Modern English translation of the Holy Bible. That means that you may freely copy it in any form, including electronic and print formats. The World English Bible is based on the American Standard Version of the Holy Bible first published in 1901, the Biblia Hebraica Stutgartensa Old Testament, and the Greek Majority Text New Testament. It is available for free download as an e-book from the Gutenberg Project, www.gutenberg.org, or from other Internet sources.

Edward F. LeGault

About the author

Edward F. LeGault was born in the Pacific Northwest. Raised in a logging family by two loving parents, he had ample time to enjoy the great outdoors.

He attended Washington State University. When the Vietnam Era draft was over he enlisted in the U.S. Navy which resulted in his education and training in just about all things electronics and computers.

After his six year enlistment, which included about 4 years seven months on the USS Nimitz (CVN-68), he worked for a variety of high tech computer companies including Logisticon, Tandem Computers and Compaq.

After being riffed, or down-sized, he went back to college, *again*, and graduated with honors with dual degrees in Management & Ethics and Bible & Theology from William Jessup University and San Jose Christian College.

His many careers have included retail sales, sailor, electronics technician, computer engineer, customer service representative, teacher, photographer, private armed security officer, tutor, and writer.

His hobbies, when not writing, include fishing, cooking, hiking/walking, reading, camping, amateur radio (call sign NX6ED), and traveling. Ed has traveled throughout Western Europe and the Middle East (mostly courtesy of the U.S. Navy). As of this writing, he has visited or lived in every state in the union except Maine, Louisiana and Alaska.

Edward F. LeGault

Ed and his wife retired to the Pacific Northwest after about three decades of living in California. He now lives not far from his original home town. Being retired means working on the homestead, tutoring (English, Reading and Math), traveling with his wife and encouraging his daughter in her art business, when he is not writing.

Edward F. LeGault

Copies of this book may be purchased at Amazon dot com.

Schools, libraries, churches and other institutions wishing to purchase larger quantities may contact the author through:

www.SerenityValleyPublishing.com

www.ingramcontent.com/pod-product-compliance
Lightning Source LLC
Chambersburg PA
CBHW072015040426
42447CB00009B/1641